12 Project Management Principles

The Time Machine Tale

(A PMP® and CAPM® Exam Study Aid)

PHILL AKINWALE, CSM, PSM, PSPO, PAL, SPS, PMI-ACP, PMP

12 Project Management Principles
Published by Praizion Media
P.O Box 22241, Mesa, AZ 85277
E-mail: info@praizion.com
www.praizion.com

Author:
Phillip Akinwale, MSc, OPM3, PMP, PMI-ACP, PSM, CSM, SPS, PAL

Copyright © 2023 Praizion Media

All rights reserved. No part of this publication may be reproduced, transmitted in any form or by any means including but not limited to electronic, recording, manual, mechanical, recording, photograph, photocopy, or stored in any retrieval system, without the prior written permission of the publisher.

ISBN 978-1-934579-25-1

The author and publisher make no warranties or representation that use of this publication will result in passing professional Agile or Scrum exams or about the completeness and accuracy of the contents. The author and publisher accept no liability, losses or damages of any kind caused or alleged to be caused directly or indirectly by this publication.

CONTENTS

- CHAPTER 0: INTRODUCTION 3
- CHAPTER 1: STEWARDSHIP 5
- CHAPTER 2: TEAM 13
- CHAPTER 3: STAKEHOLDERS 21
- CHAPTER 4: VALUE 30
- CHAPTER 5: SYSTEMS THINKING 40
- CHAPTER 6: LEADERSHIP 51
- CHAPTER 7: STAKEHOLDERS 60
- CHAPTER 8: QUALITY 70
- CHAPTER 9: COMPLEXITY 80
- CHAPTER 10: COMPLEXITY 92
- CHAPTER 11: COMPLEXITY 101
- CHAPTER 12: CHANGE 112
- CHAPTER SEVEN: QUIZ TIME 125
- ABOUT THE AUTHOR 146

PHILL AKINWALE, PMP, CSM, PSM, ACP, PAL

CHAPTER 0: INTRODUCTION

The purpose of this book is to review the 12 project management principles from the PMI®.

These principles align with the four values from The PMI® code of ethics and professional conduct,

The four values are responsibility, respect, fairness and honesty.

The principles which build on these values were identified and developed by the PMI through a global community of practitioners. There is a lot of overlap between these principles and general management principles.

12 PROJECT MANAGEMENT PRINCIPLES

In summary, the principles are as follows:

1. Be a diligent, respectful, and caring steward
2. Create a collaborative team environment
3. Effectively engage with stakeholders
4. Focus on value
5. Recognize, evaluate, and respond to system interactions
6. Demonstrate leadership behaviors
7. Tailor based on context
8. Build quality into processes and deliverables
9. Navigate complexity
10. Optimize risk responses
11. Embrace adaptability and resiliency
12. Enable change to achieve the envisioned future state

In the next number of sections, we will expand on these principles which are designed to provide guidance and best practices for project managers to ensure project success. Here is an expanded breakdown of each principle:

CHAPTER 1: STEWARDSHIP

PRINCIPLE 1: BE A DILIGENT RESPECTFUL AND CARING STEWARD

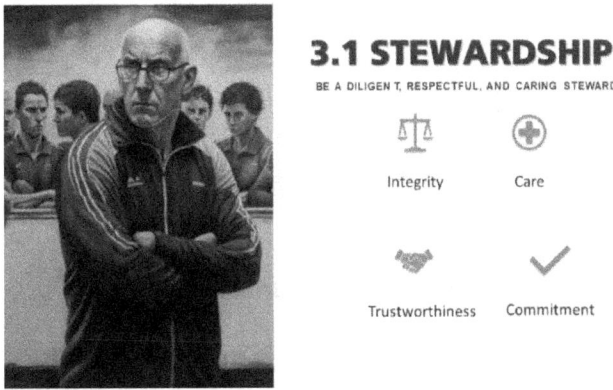

Be a Diligent, Respectful, and Caring Steward: This principle emphasizes the importance of project managers acting as stewards for the resources and stakeholders involved in the project. They must act diligently, respectfully, and with care to ensure the project's success.

Key Concepts:
- Stewards behave responsibly to carry out activities with integrity, care and trustworthiness.
- stakeholders are responsible to maintain compliance with internal and external guidelines.

- Stewardship includes integrity, care, trustworthiness, and compliance.

- Stewards should behave honestly and ethically in all engagements and communications. They should not tell half-truths or withhold information that stakeholders are Privy to.

- Stewards are fiduciaries (caretakers) of the organizational matters entrusted to them.

- Stewards represent themselves, their roles, their project team and the authority accurately both inside and outside of the organization.

- Stewards comply with laws. This refers to compliance. Rules, regulations and laws should be obeyed and followed.

The Time Machine Project (Stewardship)

Mary, a skilled and dedicated project manager, found herself at the helm of a groundbreaking project—a time machine. Her client, Dr. Zakari, a brilliant yet demanding scientist, had an insatiable desire to explore the mysteries of time. With billions of dollars at his disposal, he expected nothing short of perfection. Mary understood the importance of being a diligent, respectful, and caring steward of the project. She meticulously researched time travel theories, consulted experts, and developed a deep understanding of Dr. Zakari's vision. Despite the pressure, she remained committed to delivering an exceptional outcome while treating everyone involved with respect and empathy.

As Mary delved deeper into the time machine project, she discovered a startling revelation that threatened to unravel everything. In her research, she stumbled upon a hidden journal written by a former colleague of Dr. Zakari, who had worked on a similar project years ago. The journal detailed the catastrophic consequences that could arise from manipulating time and warned against the potential dangers.

With this newfound knowledge weighing heavily on her shoulders, Mary faced a moral dilemma. Should she confront Dr. Zakari with the information and risk jeopardizing the project? Or should she keep it to herself, knowing that the pursuit of his ambitions could have dire consequences?

As the days passed, Mary's internal struggle intensified. The weight of the secret burdened her every decision, clouding her judgment and causing her to question the ethics of her role. She couldn't help but envision the potential chaos and irreparable damage that the time machine could inflict upon the world.

Meanwhile, Dr. Zakari's impatience grew exponentially. He demanded progress updates daily and pushed for expedited completion of the project. His demanding nature made it difficult for Mary to find an appropriate moment to broach the sensitive topic. She feared his reaction, knowing that he had invested a significant amount of time and money into the venture.

Mary's nights became plagued with restless sleep and nightmares of catastrophic consequences. Her once-unwavering dedication to the project wavered as her conscience battled against her professional obligations. The pressure continued to mount, and she struggled to maintain a facade of calm professionalism while her internal turmoil threatened to consume her.

As the deadline for completion loomed, Mary knew that she had to make a choice. The ethical dilemma tore at her heart, but she couldn't ignore the potential risks any longer. She summoned her courage and scheduled a meeting with Dr. Zakari, prepared to reveal the unsettling truth about the dangers they faced.

Little did Mary know that her revelation would spark a firestorm of emotions and conflicts within the project team. The clash between scientific ambition and moral responsibility divided loyalties and strained relationships. Some members rallied behind Mary, supporting her decision to disclose the hidden dangers, while others accused her of sabotage and betrayal.

The tension escalated, creating a toxic environment within the team. Mary found herself caught in the crossfire, facing hostility from those who blamed her for disrupting their dreams of time travel. Her professional reputation, once unblemished, now hung by a thread as she became the focal point of blame and resentment.

The once-promising project, now tainted by controversy, faced delays and setbacks. Trust among team members crumbled, and the once united pursuit of scientific advancement turned into a battleground of conflicting interests and bitter rivalries. As Mary struggled to navigate the treacherous waters of ethical dilemmas and personal attacks, she realized that the consequences of her actions extended far beyond the boundaries of the project. The drama surrounding the time machine not only threatened careers but also had the potential to reshape the course of scientific exploration forever.

Self-Retrospective on Stewardship

To take your project leadership skills to the next level, it is essential to embrace the principles of being a diligent, respectful, and caring steward. This principle emphasizes the importance of managing resources responsibly, treating team members with respect, and cultivating a caring environment.

Here are some actionable coaching tips to embody this principle:

1. Diligent Stewardship:

    - Understand the project's resources: Take the time to thoroughly comprehend the available resources, including budget, time, and team members. Develop a comprehensive plan to optimize their utilization while considering long-term sustainability.

    - Continuously monitor and evaluate: Regularly review the project's progress, ensuring that resources are allocated effectively. Implement mechanisms for ongoing monitoring, such as regular status meetings, performance assessments, and data-driven analysis.

    - Foster a culture of accountability: Encourage individual and team accountability for resource usage. Clearly define roles, responsibilities, and expectations. Empower team members to take ownership of their tasks and deliverables.

2. Respectful Leadership:

    - Foster open communication: Create an environment where team members feel comfortable expressing their opinions, ideas, and concerns. Encourage active listening and create channels for transparent communication.

- Recognize diverse perspectives: Value the diverse backgrounds, experiences, and expertise within your team. Foster an inclusive environment that respects and appreciates different viewpoints.

- Empower and delegate: Trust your team members' capabilities and delegate tasks accordingly. Provide clear instructions, empower them to make decisions within their domain, and recognize their contributions.

3. Caring Environment:

- Support personal and professional growth: Show genuine interest in the development of your team members. Provide opportunities for training, mentorship, and skill enhancement. Help them set and achieve meaningful career goals.

- Promote work-life balance: Acknowledge the importance of work-life balance and support your team members in maintaining it. Encourage breaks, vacations, and flexible working arrangements when feasible.

- Celebrate achievements and milestones: Recognize and celebrate individual and team achievements. Acknowledge their hard work, dedication, and accomplishments. This fosters a positive and motivating work environment.

By embodying the principles of being a diligent, respectful, and caring steward, you will not only enhance the overall project outcomes but also create an environment where team members feel valued, motivated, and inspired to give their best.

CHAPTER 2: TEAM

PRINCIPLE 2: CREATE A COLLABORATIVE PROJECT TEAM ENVIRONMENT

Create a Collaborative Project Team Environment: This principle emphasizes the importance of creating a collaborative and inclusive project team environment to foster effective communication, promote trust, and enhance the team's performance.

Key Concepts:
- Project teams are made up of individuals with diverse skills knowledge and experience.
- Projects are delivered by project teams and therefore these teams should be treated with utmost care, concern and empathy.

- Project teams work with organizational and professional cultures and guidelines.

- A collaborative project team environment facilitates alignment with other cultures and guidelines to deliver desired outcomes. This principle is all about individuals and interactions over processes and tools.

The Time Machine Project (Team)

As the project progressed, the collaborative team environment that Mary had diligently fostered proved to be a catalyst for groundbreaking advancements. The experts, inspired by the open exchange of ideas, pushed the boundaries of their knowledge and explored uncharted territories.

With Mary's guidance, the team overcame obstacles that would have otherwise been insurmountable. Their collective intelligence and diverse skill sets allowed them to tackle complex challenges from multiple angles, leading to ingenious solutions. The project gained momentum, capturing the attention of the scientific community and captivating the imagination of the public.

As news of the time machine project spread, other scientists and experts from various fields expressed interest in joining the team. Mary's inclusive approach and reputation for creating a collaborative environment attracted some of the brightest minds in the world. The team grew in size and expertise, each member bringing their unique perspective and contributing to the project's success.

The breakthroughs achieved by the project team garnered widespread recognition and accolades. Mary, as the project manager, became a respected figure in the scientific community, admired for her leadership and ability to nurture a collaborative environment. The team's achievements also drew the attention of prestigious institutions and sponsors, who provided additional funding and resources to further accelerate their progress.

However, amidst the triumphs, a new challenge emerged. The increased visibility of the project attracted the attention of rival research groups and individuals seeking to exploit the potential of time travel for personal gain. Dark forces lurked in the shadows, plotting to obtain the time machine technology for their own nefarious purposes.

Unbeknownst to Mary and her team, an enigmatic organization had been monitoring their progress from the shadows. Fueled by greed and ambition, this clandestine group sought to seize control of the time machine, disregarding any potential consequences.

As Mary's team delved deeper into the project, they began to uncover hints of the dark forces at play. Mysterious incidents occurred—break-ins, stolen research data, and unexplained technological malfunctions. Suspicion and paranoia crept into the once harmonious team environment, threatening to erode the trust they had painstakingly built.

Recognizing the gravity of the situation, Mary called for an emergency meeting with her team. She shared her concerns, urging everyone to remain vigilant and united against the looming threat. Together, they devised strategies to fortify their defenses and protect their groundbreaking creation from falling into the wrong hands.

The project, once solely focused on scientific advancement, now became a race against time. Mary and her team had to balance their pursuit of knowledge with the need for secrecy and security. They honed their skills, prepared for potential confrontations, and established protocols to safeguard their research.

As the tension escalated, Mary found herself embroiled in a high-stakes game of cat and mouse, navigating a treacherous landscape of deception and betrayal. She had to make tough decisions and alliances, never knowing who could be trusted.

With the clock ticking and the stakes higher than ever, Mary and her team were determined to stay one step ahead of their adversaries. They knew that the collaborative environment they had built was their strongest defense—a collective force ready to face any challenge and protect the extraordinary discovery that held the power to reshape the course of history.

Self-Retrospective (Team)

It is vital to understand the significance of a cohesive and collaborative project team environment. Building effective teams is crucial for project success across industries. This principle emphasizes the value of collaboration, communication, and fostering an environment of trust and teamwork. Here are some advanced coaching tips to create a collaborative project team environment:

1. Establish clear team goals and objectives:

    - Clearly define the project goals, objectives, and expectations with the team. Ensure that everyone understands their roles and responsibilities in achieving these goals.

    - Encourage the team to set their own goals that align with the project objectives. Foster a sense of ownership and commitment to these goals.

2. Foster open and transparent communication:

- Promote a culture of open and honest communication within the team. Encourage team members to share their thoughts, concerns, and ideas freely.

- Provide multiple channels for communication, such as team meetings, virtual collaboration tools, and one-on-one discussions. Regularly solicit feedback from the team and address any issues promptly.

3. Encourage collaboration and knowledge sharing:

    - Facilitate collaboration by creating opportunities for team members to work together and share their expertise. Implement collaborative tools and platforms that enable seamless communication and document sharing.

    - Encourage cross-functional collaboration by organizing workshops, brainstorming sessions, or knowledge-sharing events. This will foster a culture of learning and innovation within the team.

4. Build trust and mutual respect:

    - Lead by example and demonstrate trustworthiness. Be transparent, honest, and reliable in your actions and communication.

- Encourage team members to trust one another by promoting open dialogue and creating a safe environment where ideas can be freely expressed without fear of judgment.

- Recognize and appreciate the unique contributions of each team member. Encourage a culture of respect and inclusion, where everyone's voice is heard and valued.

5. Foster a team-oriented mindset:

    - Encourage a sense of camaraderie and collaboration among team members. Promote a team-oriented mindset by emphasizing collective success over individual achievements.

    - Encourage cooperation and support among team members. Encourage them to help one another, share knowledge, and collaborate on problem-solving.

6. Resolve conflicts constructively:

    - Conflict is inevitable in any team environment. Teach team members conflict resolution techniques, such as active listening, seeking common ground, and finding win-win solutions.

    - Act as a mediator when conflicts arise, ensuring that all parties are heard and facilitating a resolution that benefits the team and the project.

7. Empower and delegate:

    - Empower team members by delegating responsibilities and providing them with the necessary authority to make decisions within their areas of expertise.

    - Trust your team members' capabilities and allow them to take ownership of their work. Provide guidance and support when needed, but also give them space to demonstrate their skills and creativity.

By creating a collaborative project team environment, you will harness the collective intelligence, creativity, and motivation of your team members. This will result in enhanced productivity, higher-quality deliverables, and a positive team culture that fuels project success.

CHAPTER 3: STAKEHOLDERS

PRINCIPLE 3: EFFECTIVELY ENGAGE WITH STAKEHOLDERS

3.3 STAKEHOLDERS
EFFECTIVELY ENGAGE WITH STAKEHOLDERS

Influence projects | Teams serve stakeholders (engagement) | Engagement enhances value

Effectively Engage with Stakeholders: This principle emphasizes the importance of effective stakeholder engagement throughout the project life cycle to ensure stakeholder expectations are met and the project's success is achieved.

Key Concepts:
- Engage stakeholders proactively into the degree needed to contribute to project success and customer satisfaction

- Stakeholders influence project performance and outcomes project teams serve other stakeholders by engaging with them

- stakeholder engagement proactively advances value delivery.

- It's all about value being delivered to the stakeholder.

The Time Machine Project (Stakeholders)

Engaging with stakeholders was a challenge in itself. Dr. Zakari's impatient and egocentric nature made him difficult to manage. Additionally, Mr. Pinkus, the meddlesome CEO, and Billy Bragg, the interfering program manager, added further complexity to stakeholder interactions.

Mary adopted a strategic approach to stakeholder engagement. She actively listened to their concerns, acknowledged their ideas, and communicated the project's progress transparently. By building relationships based on trust and mutual understanding, Mary was able to align stakeholder expectations and gain their support.

However, behind the façade of cooperation and collaboration, a storm was brewing. Unbeknownst to Mary, Dr. Zakari had developed a secret alliance with Mr. Pinkus. They conspired to exploit the time machine project for their personal gain, driven by their insatiable thirst for power and wealth.

Their clandestine meetings took place in the shadows, away from the prying eyes of the project team. Driven by their greed, they hatched a plan to manipulate the project's outcomes, steering it towards their hidden agenda. They sought to harness the power of time travel for their own personal ambitions, regardless of the potential consequences.

As the project advanced, Mary began to notice subtle changes in the dynamics of stakeholder interactions. The once transparent and collaborative atmosphere was slowly eroding. Ideas that were once valued were dismissed without consideration, and decisions were made behind closed doors, excluding key team members.

Unsettled by these shifts, Mary sensed a growing divide among the stakeholders. Rumors and whispers of secret alliances and hidden agendas reached her ears, but she couldn't be certain of their authenticity. She knew she had to investigate further to protect the integrity of the project and the trust she had built with her team.

Mary discreetly reached out to her most trusted team members, sharing her concerns and seeking their insights. Together, they embarked on a covert operation to uncover the truth. They gathered evidence, piecing together fragments of conversations, and observed suspicious interactions.

Their efforts paid off when they stumbled upon a hidden document—a leaked email exchange between Dr. Zakari and Mr. Pinkus. The email contained explicit details of their plan to manipulate the project and exploit the time machine for their own personal gain.

The revelation hit Mary like a punch to the gut. Betrayal radiated through her every fiber. The stakeholders she had worked so hard to engage with and gain their trust had conspired against her and the project's noble goals.

Faced with this newfound knowledge, Mary had to make a difficult choice. She could confront Dr. Zakari and Mr. Pinkus head-on, risking further damage to the project and the team's morale. Or she could devise a strategic countermove, using their betrayal to outmaneuver them and protect the project's integrity.

With her heart pounding, Mary summoned her team for an emergency meeting. She laid out the evidence before them, exposing the deception and the gravity of the situation. The atmosphere in the room grew tense as anger mixed with shock and disbelief.

Mary, determined to reclaim control and safeguard the project, rallied her team. She outlined a plan to outsmart the traitors and regain the trust of the stakeholders they had deceived. It would require cunning, resilience, and unwavering dedication.

As the team rallied behind Mary's leadership, they prepared for a battle that extended beyond the realms of science. Trust had been shattered, but the embers of their shared vision still burned brightly. With their eyes set on redemption and justice, they vowed to expose the betrayers, protect the time machine project, and restore the faith that had been shattered.

Self-Retrospective

Endeavor to understand the critical role stakeholders play in the success of any project. Effective stakeholder engagement is key to understanding their needs, managing expectations, and building strong relationships. This principle emphasizes the importance of proactive stakeholder engagement, communication, and collaboration. Here are some advanced coaching tips to effectively engage with stakeholders:

1. Identify and analyze stakeholders:

    - Conduct a thorough stakeholder analysis to identify all relevant stakeholders. Determine their level of influence, interest, and potential impact on the project.

    - Categorize stakeholders based on their roles, responsibilities, and relationship with the project. This will help you tailor your engagement strategies accordingly.

2. Develop a stakeholder engagement plan:

- Create a comprehensive stakeholder engagement plan that outlines the strategies, objectives, and activities for engaging with each stakeholder group.

- Define the desired outcomes of stakeholder engagement and set measurable goals to assess the effectiveness of your efforts.

3. Foster open and transparent communication:

    - Establish clear and consistent channels of communication with stakeholders. Keep them informed about project progress, milestones, risks, and changes.

    - Customize your communication style and message based on the stakeholder's preferences, level of understanding, and interest in the project.

4. Actively listen and understand stakeholder needs:

    - Practice active listening to understand stakeholder perspectives, concerns, and expectations. Demonstrate empathy and show genuine interest in their input.

    - Conduct regular stakeholder meetings, workshops, or focus groups to gather feedback and involve stakeholders in decision-making processes.

5. Manage expectations effectively:

    - Set realistic expectations with stakeholders regarding project scope, timeline, and deliverables. Clearly communicate any limitations or constraints that may impact their involvement or desired outcomes.

    - Be proactive in managing changes or deviations from the original plan. Communicate the rationale behind changes, assess their impact on stakeholders, and seek their input or buy-in when necessary.

6. Build strong relationships:

    - Cultivate positive and collaborative relationships with stakeholders. Invest time and effort in building trust, credibility, and rapport.

    - Show appreciation for their contributions and provide opportunities for them to participate in project-related activities or decision-making processes.

7. Anticipate and address stakeholder concerns:

    - Stay proactive in identifying and addressing potential stakeholder concerns or conflicts. Anticipate their needs, priorities, and potential risks that may arise during the project lifecycle.

    - Develop mitigation strategies and contingency plans to manage stakeholder concerns effectively.

8. Seek win-win solutions:

    - Strive for mutually beneficial outcomes when addressing stakeholder conflicts or competing interests. Look for creative solutions that address stakeholder needs while aligning with project objectives.

    - Negotiate and collaborate with stakeholders to find common ground and achieve consensus.

9. Leverage technology and tools:

    - Utilize stakeholder management software or collaboration tools to streamline communication and engagement processes. These tools can help you track interactions, manage stakeholder data, and ensure timely and targeted communication.

10. Continuously evaluate and adapt:

- Regularly assess the effectiveness of your stakeholder engagement efforts. Collect feedback, conduct satisfaction surveys, or measure stakeholder engagement metrics to identify areas for improvement.

- Adapt your engagement strategies based on stakeholder feedback, changing project dynamics, or evolving stakeholder needs.

By effectively engaging with stakeholders, you will not only foster stronger relationships but also gain valuable insights, support, and cooperation throughout the project lifecycle. This will contribute to better decision-making, reduced risks, and increased stakeholder satisfaction.

Next, let's explore the principle of focusing on value.

CHAPTER 4: VALUE

PRINCIPLE 4: FOCUS ON VALUE

3.4 Focus on Value: This principle emphasizes the importance of focusing on value to guide decision-making and ensure the project outcomes align with the project goals and objectives.

Key Concepts:
- In the Agile Manifesto, the primary measure of progress is working product. To be agile in our thinking and actions, we should continually evaluate and adjust project alignment to business objectives and intended benefits and value.

- Not only do we want to offer what works for the client it must deliver value. The Agile manifesto reads: "Our highest priority is to satisfy the customer through early and continuous delivery of valuable software."

- Value is the ultimate indicator of project success.

- Value can be realized throughout the project, at the end of the project or after the project is complete.

- Value is the net quantifiable benefit that the customer experiences as a result of the project output. So don't focus only on the deliverable instead keep value in the forefront.

- Project teams evaluate progress and adapt to maximize expected value.

The Time Machine Project (Value)

Mary understood that value was the driving force behind the project's success. With an overwhelming number of ideas from Dr. Zakari, prioritizing and focusing on the most valuable ones became critical. She worked closely with the team and stakeholders to define clear project objectives and establish metrics to measure value.

By continuously assessing the project's progress against these metrics, Mary ensured that every decision and action aligned with delivering maximum value to both Dr. Zakari and the end-users of the time machine.

The process of prioritizing ideas and features was not without its challenges. The team faced competing visions and differing opinions on what constituted value. Each stakeholder had their own agenda and expectations, making consensus difficult to achieve.

Mary took on the role of a mediator, facilitating open and constructive discussions among the team and stakeholders. She encouraged everyone to voice their perspectives and concerns, seeking common ground and shared objectives. Through these discussions, the team was able to gain a deeper understanding of the project's purpose and prioritize the ideas that would have the most significant impact.

As the project advanced, unexpected obstacles emerged. Technical difficulties and unanticipated complexities threatened to derail progress. Mary remained steadfast, using her strategic mindset to navigate these challenges. She leveraged the expertise of her team, seeking innovative solutions and adapting the project plan as necessary.

However, amidst the technical hurdles, a new challenge surfaced. The project's budget was stretched thin, and the financial constraints limited the team's ability to fully realize the envisioned scope. Mary found herself facing difficult decisions, balancing the desire for innovation with the need for cost-effectiveness.

She engaged in transparent conversations with the stakeholders, discussing the financial realities and the potential trade-offs. Mary emphasized the importance of delivering value within the available resources and explored alternative approaches to achieve the project's objectives.

Collaborating with the team, Mary encouraged creative problem-solving and resource optimization. They identified areas where cost savings could be made without compromising the core functionality and value of the time machine. Through ingenuity and careful planning, they managed to streamline processes, leverage existing technologies, and find efficiencies that stretched the budget further than anticipated.

Despite the challenges and constraints, Mary's relentless focus on maximizing value kept the project on track. The team's dedication and expertise shone through as they delivered incremental milestones that showcased the true potential of the time machine.

As the project gained momentum, its value became apparent to all stakeholders. Dr. Zakari, once driven by his own ambitious desires, began to see the broader implications of the project and its potential to benefit humanity. He grew increasingly appreciative of Mary's leadership and the team's unwavering commitment to delivering value.

With each successful milestone achieved, the skepticism and doubt that had surrounded the project began to dissipate. The stakeholders, once divided, found common ground in the value the project brought to their respective domains. The collaborative spirit that Mary had fostered rekindled, reinforcing their shared commitment to the project's success.

Mary's ability to align the project's objectives with the values of both Dr. Zakari and the end-users became a cornerstone of the project's achievements. It was through her relentless pursuit of value that the time machine project transcended its initial ambitions, becoming a symbol of scientific progress and a beacon of hope for a better future.

Self-Retrospective

As an experienced project manager, you understand the importance of delivering value to stakeholders and the organization. The principle of focusing on value emphasizes the need to prioritize and optimize project outcomes to maximize value creation. By adopting a value-driven approach, you can ensure that your projects align with strategic objectives and deliver tangible benefits. Here are some advanced coaching tips to help you focus on value:

1. Define clear value criteria:

   - Collaborate with stakeholders to define the key value criteria for the project. This may include financial metrics, strategic alignment, customer satisfaction, or other measurable indicators.

   - Prioritize and rank the value criteria based on their importance and relevance to the project's overall objectives.

2. Align projects with strategic objectives:

   - Understand the organization's strategic goals and ensure that your projects directly contribute to their achievement. Align project outcomes with the strategic priorities of the organization.

   - Regularly communicate the strategic relevance of the project to stakeholders, highlighting how it supports the organization's long-term vision.

3. Conduct robust feasibility studies:

   - Before initiating a project, conduct thorough feasibility studies to assess its viability, potential benefits, risks, and alignment with organizational goals.

- Evaluate alternative solutions or approaches to determine the most value-driven option. Consider the trade-offs between cost, quality, time, and other factors.

4. Implement value management techniques:

    - Utilize value management techniques such as value engineering, value analysis, or value stream mapping to identify opportunities for optimizing project value.

    - Continuously evaluate project activities, processes, and deliverables to identify areas where value can be enhanced, risks mitigated, or costs reduced.

5. Continuously measure and track value:

    - Establish key performance indicators (KPIs) and metrics to measure project value throughout its lifecycle. Monitor and track progress against these metrics regularly.

    - Communicate value-related metrics to stakeholders to demonstrate the project's impact and the value created. This could include metrics such as return on investment (ROI), cost savings, revenue generation, customer satisfaction ratings, or other relevant measures.

6. Engage stakeholders in value discussions:

   - Involve stakeholders in discussions about project value and benefits. Seek their input and perspectives on how the project can deliver greater value or address their specific needs.

   - Communicate the value proposition of the project in a compelling manner, emphasizing the benefits and outcomes that stakeholders can expect.

7. Continuously seek opportunities for value optimization:

   - Encourage a culture of innovation and continuous improvement within your project team. Foster an environment where team members are empowered to identify and implement value optimization initiatives.

   - Regularly evaluate the project's progress and performance, identifying opportunities for value enhancement. This may involve reevaluating project scope, adjusting priorities, or exploring new technologies or approaches.

8. Manage changes with value in mind:

- When changes occur during the project, assess their impact on value delivery. Prioritize changes that align with value creation and have the highest potential for positive impact.

- Communicate the implications of changes on value to stakeholders, ensuring transparency and alignment throughout the change management process.

9. Foster a value-focused mindset:

    - Instill a value-focused mindset within the project team, encouraging them to always consider the value proposition in their decision-making processes.

    - Promote a culture of accountability and ownership, where each team member understands their role in delivering value and is committed to achieving it.

10. Learn from past projects:

    - Reflect on past projects and identify lessons learned regarding value delivery. Capture best practices, success stories, and areas for improvement to inform future projects.

    - Incorporate these learnings into your project management processes and share them with the team to foster continuous growth and value optimization.

By focusing on value throughout the project lifecycle, you can ensure that your efforts align with strategic objectives, meet stakeholder expectations, and maximize the benefits delivered. This value-driven approach will position you as a leader who consistently delivers meaningful outcomes and drives organizational success.

Next, let's explore the principle of recognizing, evaluating, and responding to system interactions.

CHAPTER 5: SYSTEMS THINKING

PRINCIPLE 5: RECOGNIZE, EVALUATE AND RESPOND TO SYSTEMS INTERACTION

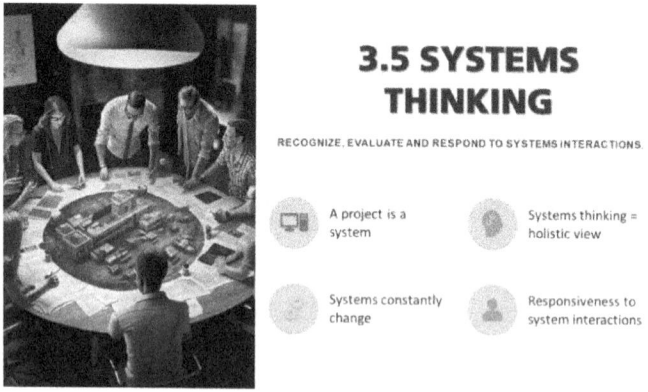

3.5 Recognize, Evaluate, and Respond to System Interactions: This principle emphasizes the importance of recognizing, evaluating, and responding to system interactions that impact the project's success. This includes the interdependent relationships between the project and other systems.

Key Concepts:
- A project is a system within a wider external system. It is a system of interdependent and interacting domains of activity.

- Recognize evaluate and respond to the dynamic circumstances within and surrounding the project in a holistic way, to positively affect project performance.

- Systems thinking involves seeing the project and its environment holistically, observing how project paths interact with each other and with external systems.

- Systems are constantly changing requiring consistent attention to internal and external conditions.

- Being responsive to systems interactions is a factor that enables teams get the best project outcomes.

The Time Machine Project (Systems Thinking)

As the project progressed, Mary encountered various system interactions that demanded her attention. The complexities of time travel required her to recognize and evaluate the interdependencies and interactions between different project components.

Through careful analysis and with the support of the project team, Mary identified potential risks and opportunities stemming from these interactions. She developed proactive response plans, ensuring that any potential challenges were addressed promptly and effectively.

The intricacies of time travel brought forth a multitude of complex interactions. Mary worked closely with the team of scientists and engineers, pooling their collective expertise to understand and mitigate the risks involved. They conducted extensive simulations, modelings, and tests to evaluate the potential effects of various system interactions.

During this process, they uncovered critical interdependencies that could have far-reaching consequences if left unaddressed. The project team identified scenarios where even minor changes in one component could have ripple effects throughout the entire system, leading to catastrophic outcomes.

Recognizing the urgency and importance of managing these interactions, Mary initiated a series of collaborative workshops and brainstorming sessions. Experts from diverse fields, including physics, engineering, and computer science, came together to share insights and perspectives.

The team meticulously dissected each potential interaction, analyzing the risks and benefits associated with them. They developed comprehensive response plans, outlining strategies to mitigate risks, exploit opportunities, and optimize the overall system performance.

Mary's leadership in recognizing the significance of these interactions and fostering a collaborative environment allowed the project team to proactively address potential pitfalls. They implemented rigorous testing protocols, ensuring that the time machine's components functioned seamlessly together, reducing the likelihood of unforeseen issues arising during operation.

However, as the project neared its final stages, an unexpected and potentially catastrophic interaction came to light. Mary and her team discovered a hidden flaw in the time machine's algorithm that could lead to a destabilization of the space-time continuum.

The magnitude of this revelation sent shockwaves through the project team. Mary knew that the implications were dire and immediate action was necessary to prevent disaster. She convened an emergency meeting, gathering the best minds in the team to find a solution.

Hours turned into days as the team tirelessly worked to develop a response plan. Their collective expertise and collaboration allowed them to devise a novel approach to resolve the algorithmic flaw without compromising the project's objectives.

The project team executed the response plan with precision and urgency, implementing the necessary modifications to the time machine's algorithm. Exhaustive testing and validation ensured the stability and safety of the system.

Through their collective efforts and under Mary's guidance, the project team successfully averted the looming disaster. The incident served as a reminder of the complexities inherent in their groundbreaking endeavor and the importance of continuously evaluating and managing system interactions.

As the project reached its culmination, the meticulous attention paid to these interactions proved to be the foundation of its success. Mary's commitment to recognizing, evaluating, and addressing complex interdependencies safeguarded the integrity of the time machine and ensured its safe and effective operation.

The lessons learned from navigating these interactions became invaluable for future endeavors and further solidified Mary's reputation as a skilled and vigilant project manager. The project's success was not only a testament to scientific achievement but also a testament to the power of careful analysis and proactive planning in mitigating risks and seizing opportunities.

To be continued...

Self-Retrospective

As an advanced and visionary project manager, it is crucial to understand and address the complex system interactions that can impact project outcomes. The principle of recognizing, evaluating, and responding to system interactions highlights the need to consider the interconnectedness and interdependencies within a project and its broader context. Here are some actionable coaching tips to effectively navigate system interactions:

1. Develop systems thinking:

    - Cultivate a systems thinking mindset among your project team. Encourage them to understand the project as a complex system with multiple interrelated components.

    - Foster a holistic view of the project and its interactions with external systems, such as organizational processes, market dynamics, technological ecosystems, and regulatory frameworks.

2. Identify key system components and stakeholders:

    - Conduct a comprehensive analysis to identify the critical components of the project system and the stakeholders involved. Consider both internal and external factors that can influence project success.

- Map out the relationships, dependencies, and feedback loops among these components to visualize the system interactions.

3. Assess potential impacts and risks:

    - Evaluate the potential impacts and risks arising from system interactions. Identify both positive and negative impacts on project objectives, timelines, costs, quality, and stakeholder satisfaction.

    - Anticipate potential system bottlenecks, conflicts, or dependencies that may hinder project progress. Develop mitigation strategies to address these risks proactively.

4. Foster collaboration and coordination:

    - Encourage collaboration and coordination among stakeholders to navigate system interactions effectively. Facilitate cross-functional communication, information sharing, and collaboration platforms.

    - Establish governance structures and mechanisms to ensure that system interactions are effectively managed. This may involve establishing steering committees, regular meetings, or communication channels where stakeholders can discuss and align on system-related issues.

5. Engage with experts and specialists:

    - Identify subject matter experts or specialists who can provide valuable insights into specific system interactions. Consult with them to gain a deeper understanding of the complexities involved and to develop appropriate strategies.

    - Foster partnerships with external organizations or consultants who have expertise in the specific system domains relevant to your project.

6. Conduct impact assessments:

    - Perform thorough impact assessments to understand the potential consequences of system interactions on project outcomes. This includes assessing the ripple effects of changes in one system component on others.

    - Use tools and techniques such as scenario analysis, simulation, or modeling to evaluate different scenarios and their potential impacts.

7. Adapt plans and strategies:

- Based on the assessment of system interactions, be prepared to adapt your plans and strategies accordingly. Flexibility and agility are key to navigating complex system dynamics.

- Adjust project timelines, resource allocations, or strategies to accommodate changes resulting from system interactions. Communicate these changes to stakeholders and ensure their understanding and support.

8. Establish feedback loops:

    - Implement feedback loops within the project system to continuously monitor and evaluate the impact of system interactions. Regularly assess the effectiveness of strategies in addressing these interactions and make adjustments as needed.

    - Encourage stakeholders to provide feedback and insights on the system interactions they observe. This can help identify emerging issues or opportunities that might have been overlooked.

9. Communicate system impacts and dependencies:

    - Ensure effective communication of system impacts and dependencies to stakeholders.

Clearly articulate how changes or decisions in one system component can affect others and the overall project.

- Use visual aids, diagrams, or presentations to illustrate the interconnectedness of systems and the potential consequences of actions or decisions.

10. Continuously learn and improve:

    - Foster a culture of continuous learning and improvement regarding system interactions. Encourage project team members to reflect on lessons learned from past projects and apply them to enhance future project outcomes.

    - Promote knowledge sharing and collaboration across projects to leverage collective experiences and expertise in managing system interactions effectively.

By recognizing, evaluating, and responding to system interactions, you can navigate the complexities and interdependencies inherent in projects. This proactive approach will enable you to anticipate challenges, capitalize on opportunities, and optimize project outcomes in a dynamic and interconnected environment.

Next, let's explore the principle of demonstrating leadership behaviors.

CHAPTER 6: LEADERSHIP

PRINCIPLE 6: DEMONSTRATE LEADERSHIP BEHAVIORS

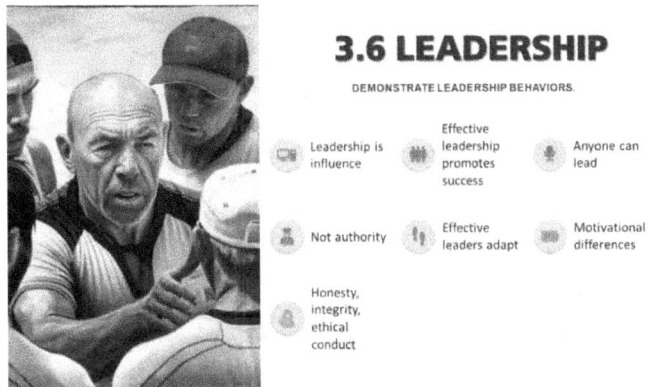

3.6 Demonstrate Leadership Behaviors: This principle emphasizes the importance of demonstrating effective leadership behaviors to ensure project success. This includes creating a vision, motivating the team, and empowering team members to achieve project goals.

Key Concepts:
So how do we demonstrate leadership behaviors? My mentor john maxwell always says "the true measure of leadership is influence nothing more nothing less". He also says "he who thinks he leadeth but has no one following after him is only taking a walk"

- Demonstrating leadership behaviors means influencing with integrity, trust, empathy, passion, vision and servant leadership mindedness.

- Great leaders adapt their leadership approach and style to fit the unique team and individuals they are working with. An example of this is the Hersey-Blanchard model. Situational leadership!

- This is where we understand individuals are different. Effective leadership promotes project success and contributes to positive project outcomes.

- Leadership is not authority. Granted, authority is the starting point for a leader, but leadership is much more than just authority!

- Effective leaders adapt their style to the situation. Effective leaders recognize differences in motivation among project team members.

The Time Machine Project (Leadership)

Leadership behaviors were paramount in guiding the project towards success. Mary set a positive example by being an effective communicator, problem solver, and decision-maker. She inspired the team through her unwavering determination, resilience, and empathy.

Mary nurtured a culture of trust, where team members felt empowered to take ownership of their tasks and share their ideas openly. She provided guidance and support when needed, fostering personal and professional growth within the team.

As a leader, Mary recognized the importance of effective communication. She maintained transparent and open channels of communication, ensuring that information flowed freely among team members and stakeholders. Regular meetings and progress updates allowed everyone to stay informed, aligned, and engaged in the project's objectives.

In addition to communication, Mary excelled at problem-solving. When challenges arose, she encouraged the team to approach them as opportunities for innovation and growth. She facilitated brainstorming sessions, encouraging diverse perspectives and creative thinking. By fostering a collaborative environment, Mary empowered the team to tackle complex problems and find effective solutions.

Making critical decisions was another aspect of Mary's leadership. She carefully weighed the available information, considering the input of the team and stakeholders, to make informed choices. Mary understood the importance of decisive action, especially in a project as ambitious as the time machine. Her ability to make tough decisions, even under pressure, instilled confidence and provided a clear direction for the team to follow.

Mary's leadership extended beyond technical expertise. She recognized the human element of the project and showed empathy towards her team members. She understood the pressures they faced and actively supported their well-being. Whether it was recognizing their achievements, providing mentorship, or addressing any concerns, Mary ensured that the team felt valued and supported throughout the project.

By demonstrating these leadership behaviors, Mary fostered a sense of camaraderie and unity within the team. Their shared vision and trust in her leadership propelled them to overcome obstacles and achieve remarkable milestones.

As the project reached its final stages, the team's dedication and collective effort became evident to all stakeholders. Dr. Zakari, initially skeptical and demanding, recognized the impact of Mary's leadership on the project's success. He publicly acknowledged her role and the exceptional performance of the team.

The project's achievements under Mary's leadership garnered admiration and respect from the scientific community. Mary's reputation as a skilled project manager and leader spread beyond the confines of the time machine project. She became a role model for aspiring project managers, inspiring them to cultivate leadership behaviors and embrace the responsibilities that come with guiding ambitious endeavors.

As the time machine project nears its completion, Mary's leadership behaviors continue to shape its final stages. The trust she has built, the effective communication she maintains, and her ability to inspire and problem-solve propel the team towards a successful outcome.

Self-Retrospective

your leadership plays a crucial role in driving project success. The principle of demonstrating leadership behaviors emphasizes the need for project managers to inspire, motivate, and guide their teams toward achieving project goals. Here are some actionable coaching tips to enhance your leadership behaviors:

1. Lead by example:

    - Be a role model for your team by consistently demonstrating the behaviors and values you expect from them. Show integrity, professionalism, and a strong work ethic in all your actions.

    - Take ownership of your responsibilities, admit mistakes when necessary, and learn from them. Display a positive attitude and resilience in the face of challenges.

2. Communicate effectively:

    - Develop strong communication skills to convey information, expectations, and feedback clearly. Adapt your communication style to different audiences and situations.

- Listen actively to team members, stakeholders, and other project participants. Seek their input, address their concerns, and encourage open and honest dialogue.

3. Inspire and motivate:

    - Inspire your team by sharing a compelling vision for the project. Connect their work to the larger purpose and goals of the organization, highlighting the impact of their contributions.

    - Recognize and celebrate team achievements and individual efforts. Provide constructive feedback and encouragement to boost motivation and foster a positive and productive work environment.

4. Empower and delegate:

    - Empower your team members by providing them with the necessary resources, authority, and autonomy to make decisions and take ownership of their work.

    - Delegate tasks and responsibilities effectively, considering individual strengths and development opportunities. Provide guidance and support while allowing team members to grow and excel in their roles.

5. Foster collaboration and teamwork:

    - Create a collaborative and inclusive project team environment where diverse perspectives are valued. Encourage teamwork, knowledge sharing, and mutual respect among team members.

    - Facilitate effective collaboration by establishing clear roles, responsibilities, and communication channels. Encourage cross-functional cooperation and break down silos.

6. Coach and mentor:

    - Take on the role of a coach and mentor for your team members. Provide guidance, support, and development opportunities to help them enhance their skills and reach their full potential.

    - Offer constructive feedback, conduct regular performance evaluations, and identify areas for improvement. Create a culture of continuous learning and growth.

7. Make informed decisions:

    - Demonstrate sound judgment and decision-making skills by gathering and analyzing relevant information. Consider the input of key stakeholders and subject matter experts.

- Communicate the rationale behind your decisions and ensure transparency in the decision-making process. Involve the team in decision-making whenever possible to foster a sense of ownership.

8. Manage conflicts and challenges:

    - Proactively address conflicts and challenges that arise within the project team. Encourage open communication and facilitate conflict resolution through effective negotiation and collaboration.

    - Identify and mitigate risks and obstacles that may hinder project progress. Stay calm under pressure and maintain a solutions-oriented approach.

9. Continuously develop leadership skills:

    - Invest in your own professional development as a leader. Stay updated on the latest project management methodologies, industry trends, and leadership best practices.

    - Seek opportunities to enhance your leadership skills through training, workshops, conferences, or networking events. Embrace new challenges and learn from experiences.

10. Inspire a culture of innovation:

- Foster a culture of innovation within your project team by encouraging creativity, experimentation, and continuous improvement. Embrace new ideas and encourage team members to think outside the box.

- Celebrate and recognize innovative thinking and solutions. Create an environment where calculated risks are encouraged, and failures are seen as learning opportunities.

By demonstrating strong leadership behaviors, you will inspire your team to perform at their best, foster a collaborative and positive work environment, and drive project success. Your leadership will be instrumental in achieving project objectives, overcoming challenges, and creating a high-performing project team.

Next, let's explore the principle of tailoring based on context.

CHAPTER 7: STAKEHOLDERS

PRINCIPLE 7: TAILOR BASED ON CONTEXT

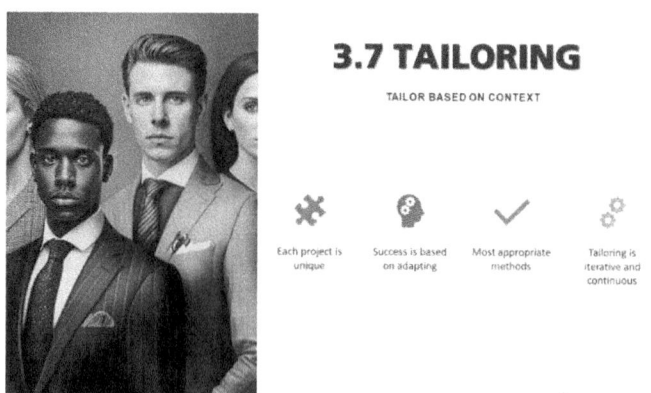

3.7 Tailor Based on Context: This principle emphasizes the importance of tailoring project management approaches based on the project's context. This includes considering project characteristics, stakeholders, and the environment in which the project is being executed. Tailoring based on context means you are tailoring with a unique circumstance in mind, understanding that each project is unique.

Key Concepts:
- No two projects are exactly the same! The time frame in which the project is taking place, the organization,

the stakeholders, all of these make for a unique experience project by project.

- So tailoring is the job of the project manager and the team working together collaboratively but doing so in context.

- Understanding that projects have similarities but are not exactly the same is important.

- Project success is based on adapting to the unique context of the project to determine the most appropriate methods of producing the desired outcomes.

- Tailoring the approach is iterative and therefore is a continuous process throughout the project.

- Adaptive methods, predictive methods, hybrid methods, it is these considerations that are being referred to in the context of tailoring.

The Time Machine Project (Tailoring)

Understanding that every project is unique, Mary recognized the importance of tailoring project management approaches based on the context. She adapted methodologies, processes, and techniques to suit the specific needs of the time machine project.

By considering the project's scope, stakeholders, and organizational culture, Mary ensured that the project management approach remained agile and flexible throughout, accommodating any necessary adjustments.

Mary began by conducting a thorough assessment of the project's context. She considered the project's complexity, timeline, and resources, as well as the expectations and preferences of the stakeholders involved. This allowed her to determine the most suitable project management methodology to employ.

Recognizing the need for adaptability in a rapidly evolving project like the time machine, Mary chose to adopt an agile project management approach. Agile methodologies provided the flexibility and responsiveness required to address the uncertainties and changing requirements inherent in such a groundbreaking endeavor.

Under Mary's guidance, the team embraced agile principles, such as iterative development, frequent feedback loops, and continuous improvement. They implemented short sprints, allowing for rapid prototyping and validation of ideas. The team regularly reviewed progress and adjusted their course as needed, leveraging their collective expertise to drive the project forward effectively.

In addition to an agile approach, Mary recognized the importance of tailoring specific processes and techniques to suit the project's needs. She leveraged best practices from different project management methodologies, combining them to create a hybrid approach tailored to the time machine project.

For example, Mary incorporated elements of lean project management to optimize resource utilization and minimize waste. She introduced kanban boards to visualize and track the flow of work, promoting transparency and efficiency. This helped the team prioritize tasks and maintain a steady workflow.

Mary also understood that effective stakeholder management was crucial for project success. She tailored her communication strategies and engagement approaches to suit the preferences and expectations of the diverse stakeholders involved. Some stakeholders required detailed technical updates, while others preferred high-level summaries of progress. Mary ensured that each stakeholder received the information they needed in a format that resonated with them.

Throughout the project, Mary remained vigilant in assessing the effectiveness of the tailored project management approach. She sought feedback from the team and stakeholders, actively listened to their suggestions, and made adjustments accordingly. This iterative approach allowed her to fine-tune the project management processes, ensuring that they continued to meet the evolving needs of the project.

By tailoring the project management approach to the context of the time machine project, Mary and her team achieved remarkable results. They maintained a nimble and adaptable mindset, quickly responding to changes and seizing opportunities. The tailored approach allowed them to navigate the complexities and uncertainties of the project, ensuring its success while meeting stakeholder expectations.

As the time machine project approached its final countdown, Mary's ability to tailor project management based on context would prove invaluable. The adaptability she demonstrated would be crucial in addressing the unique challenges and requirements that lay ahead.

Self-Retrospective

As an experienced project manager, you understand that a one-size-fits-all approach does not work for every project. The principle of tailoring based on context emphasizes the importance of adapting project management practices to suit the unique characteristics, requirements, and constraints of each project. Here are some advanced coaching tips to help you tailor your approach based on the project context:

1. Understand the project context:

    - Take the time to thoroughly understand the project context, including its goals, objectives, stakeholders, organizational culture, and external influences. Consider factors such as industry, technology, regulatory requirements, and market conditions.

- Identify the specific challenges, opportunities, and risks associated with the project. Assess the level of complexity, uncertainty, and uniqueness involved.

2. Select the appropriate project management approach:

    - Choose the most suitable project management approach that aligns with the project context. This could be a traditional waterfall approach, an agile methodology, a hybrid model, or any other tailored approach.

    - Consider factors such as project size, complexity, level of stakeholder involvement, scope flexibility, and the need for iterative feedback and adaptation. Select the approach that best addresses the project's unique characteristics and aligns with organizational goals.

3. Customize project processes and tools:

    - Tailor project processes and methodologies to fit the project's specific needs. Identify the necessary process areas, activities, and deliverables based on the project's scope, timeline, and complexity.

- Select and adapt project management tools and technologies that enhance project efficiency and effectiveness. Leverage software, communication platforms, and collaboration tools that align with the project's requirements.

4. Define project roles and responsibilities:

    - Clearly define project roles and responsibilities based on the project's context and team dynamics. Tailor the project team structure, ensuring that each member's skills and expertise are well-utilized.

    - Assign ownership of tasks and decision-making authority based on individual strengths and project requirements. Foster a sense of accountability and collaboration among team members.

5. Customize communication and reporting:

    - Tailor the communication and reporting approach to suit the project's context and stakeholder needs. Determine the frequency, format, and channels of communication based on the project's complexity, size, and stakeholder preferences.

- Adapt communication strategies to ensure that project progress, risks, and issues are effectively communicated to stakeholders. Provide relevant and timely information that aligns with their interests and needs.

6. Adjust project planning and control:

    - Customize the project planning and control processes based on the project context. Determine the appropriate level of detail and rigor required for project planning, scheduling, and resource management.

    - Tailor the project monitoring and control mechanisms to suit the project's complexity and stakeholder expectations. Define key performance indicators (KPIs) and metrics that accurately measure project progress and success.

7. Consider cultural and organizational factors:

    - Take into account cultural and organizational factors that influence project management practices. Respect and adapt to the cultural norms, communication styles, and decision-making processes prevalent within the organization and project environment.

- Understand the organization's governance frameworks, policies, and procedures, and align the project management approach accordingly. Ensure compliance with regulatory requirements and industry standards.

8. Continuously assess and refine:

- Regularly assess the effectiveness of the tailored project management approach. Solicit feedback from stakeholders, team members, and project sponsors to identify areas for improvement and refinements.

- Continuously adapt and refine the project management approach based on lessons learned, feedback, and changing project circumstances. Foster a culture of continuous improvement and learning.

9. Seek expert guidance when needed:

- If you encounter unique challenges or unfamiliar project contexts, seek guidance from experts, consultants, or mentors who have experience in similar situations. Leverage their expertise to make informed decisions and ensure effective tailoring.

10. Document lessons learned:

    - Document the lessons learned from tailoring project management approaches in different contexts. Capture best practices, challenges faced, and strategies that proved successful.

    - Share these lessons learned with the project team and organizational stakeholders to promote knowledge sharing and to enhance future project management practices.

By tailoring your project management approach based on the project context, you will increase the likelihood of project success. This tailored approach demonstrates your ability to adapt to different situations, maximize project outcomes, and effectively address project-specific challenges.

Next, let's explore the principle of building quality into processes and deliverables.

CHAPTER 8: QUALITY

3.8 Principle 8: Build quality into processes and deliverables

3.8 Build Quality into Processes and Deliverables: This principle emphasizes the importance of building quality into project processes and deliverables. This includes a focus on preventing defects, continuous improvement, and ensuring that the project meets the quality requirements.

Key Concepts:
- Technical excellence and good design enhances agility! This is all about quality,
- Project quality is all about satisfying stakeholder expectations and fulfilling project and product requirements.

- Quality is three things: fitness for use, conforming to requirements, and customer satisfaction (which trumps everything else).

- Quality focuses on meeting acceptance criteria for deliverables. Project quality entails ensuring project processes are appropriate and as effective as possible. Remember that at the end of the sprint, the team tunes and adjusts its behavior.

- This is a quality job. Quality is of paramount importance to the project manager.

The Time Machine Project (Quality)

Mary understood that building quality into processes was essential for the success of the time machine project. She knew that delivering a high-quality product would not only meet Dr. Zakari's expectations but also ensure the safety and reliability of the time machine.

She implemented rigorous quality control measures from the project's inception. Mary collaborated with the team to establish clear quality objectives and standards. They developed robust processes and guidelines for each phase of the project, ensuring that all deliverables met the required quality criteria.

To promote a culture of quality, Mary emphasized the importance of attention to detail and adherence to established procedures. She conducted regular quality audits and inspections, involving both the project team and external experts, to identify any deviations or potential improvements.

Continuous improvement was a fundamental aspect of the quality management process. Mary encouraged the team to learn from past experiences and implement lessons learned to enhance future project activities. She fostered an environment where constructive feedback was welcomed, allowing for ongoing refinements and optimizations.

Mary recognized that quality should be built into the project's processes rather than treated as an afterthought. She collaborated with the team to define quality checkpoints at critical milestones, ensuring that each deliverable underwent thorough evaluation and validation before proceeding to the next stage.

To ensure adherence to quality standards, Mary championed the use of rigorous testing and validation procedures. The team conducted extensive testing to verify the functionality, reliability, and safety of the time machine. They developed test plans, executed test cases, and meticulously recorded and analyzed the results.

Through these testing efforts, the team identified and addressed any defects, inconsistencies, or vulnerabilities in the time machine's design and functionality. They iteratively refined the system, ensuring that it met the highest quality standards and specifications.

Mary also emphasized the importance of stakeholder involvement in the quality management process. She actively sought feedback from stakeholders and end-users, incorporating their perspectives into the quality assurance activities. By incorporating their expectations and requirements, the team was able to deliver a product that met their needs and exceeded their expectations.

As the project neared its final stages, Mary ensured that the quality management efforts remained robust and vigilant. She instilled a sense of accountability and ownership among the team, emphasizing the importance of delivering a time machine that not only worked flawlessly but also met the stringent quality standards set forth.

By building quality into processes, Mary and her team not only created a time machine that was groundbreaking in its capabilities but also instilled confidence in its performance and reliability. The commitment to quality permeated every aspect of the project, from design and development to testing and validation.

As the ultimate leap approached, Mary's dedication to building quality into processes would prove instrumental in ensuring the success and long-term viability of the time machine. The project stood as a testament to the power of rigorous quality management and its impact on delivering exceptional outcomes.

Self-Retrospective

As an advanced project manager, it is essential to prioritize quality throughout the project lifecycle. The principle of building quality into processes and deliverables emphasizes the importance of establishing robust quality management practices to ensure that project outputs meet or exceed stakeholder expectations. Here are some actionable coaching tips to build quality into your project processes and deliverables:

1. Define quality objectives:

- Clearly define quality objectives that align with stakeholder expectations and project requirements. Identify the key quality criteria and performance indicators that will be used to assess the success of the project.

- Involve relevant stakeholders in the process of defining quality objectives to ensure their buy-in and alignment with their needs and expectations.

2. Incorporate quality planning:

    - Develop a comprehensive quality management plan that outlines the processes, tools, and techniques to be used throughout the project. This plan should address how quality will be planned, executed, monitored, and controlled.

    - Identify the specific quality standards, methodologies, and best practices that will be applied to ensure consistent and high-quality deliverables.

3. Engage stakeholders in quality management:

    - Involve stakeholders in the quality management process by seeking their input, feedback, and validation. Regularly communicate with stakeholders to ensure their expectations are understood and incorporated into the quality management approach.

- Establish mechanisms for stakeholders to provide feedback on deliverables and participate in quality reviews and inspections.

4. Implement quality assurance activities:

- Conduct regular quality assurance activities to ensure that project processes are being followed correctly and that deliverables meet the defined quality standards. This may include audits, inspections, reviews, and tests.

- Assign dedicated resources or a quality assurance team to monitor and evaluate project activities, processes, and deliverables. Provide them with the necessary authority and independence to perform their roles effectively.

5. Emphasize preventive actions:

- Take a proactive approach to quality management by focusing on preventive actions rather than reactive ones. Identify potential quality risks and issues early in the project and develop mitigation strategies to address them.

- Implement quality control measures to detect and correct deviations from quality standards before they impact project outcomes.

6. Implement quality control measures:

    - Establish rigorous quality control processes to monitor and evaluate the quality of project deliverables. This may include inspections, testing, peer reviews, and verification activities.

    - Implement tools and techniques to measure and analyze quality performance, such as statistical process control, benchmarking, or defect tracking systems. Use these insights to identify trends, areas for improvement, and opportunities to enhance quality.

7. Foster a culture of quality:

    - Create a project team culture that values and prioritizes quality. Communicate the importance of quality to team members and stakeholders, and ensure that it is integrated into every aspect of the project.

    - Encourage a mindset of continuous improvement and learning from quality-related feedback and lessons learned. Celebrate and recognize achievements in quality to reinforce its significance.

8. Provide training and support:

    - Ensure that project team members have the necessary knowledge, skills, and tools to deliver quality outcomes. Provide training and support in quality management methodologies, tools, and techniques.

    - Foster a learning environment where team members can develop their quality-related competencies and share knowledge and experiences.

9. Monitor and measure quality performance:

    - Establish a robust system for monitoring and measuring quality performance throughout the project. Regularly collect and analyze quality data to assess compliance with quality standards, identify trends, and drive improvement.

    - Use key quality metrics and indicators to communicate the project's quality performance to stakeholders. Provide regular reports on quality status, trends, and actions taken to address quality issues.

10. Continuously improve quality processes:

- Foster a culture of continuous improvement in quality management. Encourage team members to identify and share opportunities for enhancing quality processes and deliverables.

- Conduct periodic reviews of the quality management approach and adapt it based on lessons learned, feedback from stakeholders, and emerging best practices.

By building quality into processes and deliverables, you demonstrate your commitment to delivering successful projects that meet or exceed stakeholder expectations. This focus on quality will enhance stakeholder satisfaction, reduce rework and defects, and contribute to the long-term success and reputation of your projects.

Next, let's explore the principle of navigating complexity.

CHAPTER 9: COMPLEXITY

PRINCIPLE 9: NAVIGATE COMPLEXITY

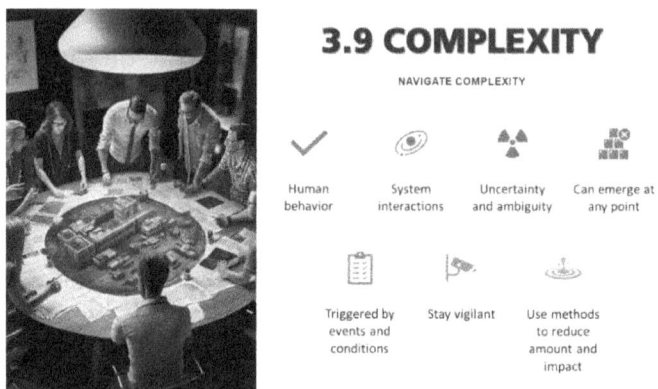

3.9 Navigate Complexity: This principle emphasizes the importance of navigating project complexity. This includes the ability to handle uncertainty, ambiguity, and managing project risk.

Key Concepts:
- Complexity is the result of human behavior, system interactions, uncertainty and ambiguity.
- Complexity can emerge at any point during the project. Complexity can be introduced by events or conditions that affect value, scope, communications, stakeholders' risk and technological innovation.

- Project teams can stay vigilant in identifying elements of complexity and use a variety of models and methods to reduce the amount of impact of complexity.

The Time Machine Project (Complexity)

The time machine project presented unprecedented levels of complexity. The scientific theories involved, the advanced technology required, and the demanding expectations of Dr. Zakari posed significant challenges for Mary and her team.

To navigate this complexity, Mary employed a systematic approach. She conducted comprehensive risk assessments to identify potential complexities and their associated impacts. She collaborated with experts in relevant fields, leveraging their specialized knowledge to overcome hurdles.

Mary fostered an environment of collaboration and knowledge sharing within the team, encouraging creative problem-solving and exploration of innovative solutions. She broke down complex tasks into manageable components, promoting clarity and focus.

With each challenge that arose, Mary and her team embraced the complexity head-on. They researched, consulted experts, and engaged in rigorous discussions to gain a deep understanding of the intricacies involved. By acknowledging and addressing the complexity, they were able to develop effective strategies and make informed decisions.

Recognizing that collaboration was vital, Mary facilitated regular meetings and workshops to share insights and brainstorm solutions. The team pooled their collective knowledge and expertise, combining their diverse perspectives to tackle complex issues from multiple angles. This collaborative approach not only generated creative solutions but also fostered a sense of ownership and shared responsibility among team members.

Mary also emphasized the importance of continuous learning and improvement. The complexities of the project presented opportunities for growth and innovation. By embracing the challenges and seeking new ways to navigate the complexity, Mary and her team were able to push the boundaries of their knowledge and capabilities.

Self-Retrospective

In today's dynamic and interconnected business landscape, projects often face high levels of complexity. The principle of navigating complexity emphasizes the need for project managers to understand, embrace, and effectively navigate complex environments. Here are advanced coaching tips to navigate complexity in your projects:

1. Understand the complexity landscape:

   - Gain a deep understanding of the complexity landscape surrounding your project. Identify the various interdependencies, uncertainties, and interconnected systems that impact project outcomes.

   - Analyze the internal and external factors that contribute to project complexity, such as technological advancements, regulatory requirements, market dynamics, and stakeholder expectations.

2. Embrace systems thinking:

   - Adopt a systems thinking approach to understand the intricate relationships and interactions within the project ecosystem. Consider the project as a complex system with multiple interdependent components.

   - Recognize that changes or actions in one part of the system can have ripple effects on other parts. Take a holistic view when making decisions and assessing the potential impact on the entire project.

3. Develop a comprehensive risk management strategy:

    - Proactively identify, assess, and manage risks associated with project complexity. Develop a comprehensive risk management strategy that includes risk identification, analysis, response planning, and monitoring.

    - Engage stakeholders to gain their insights on potential risks and uncertainties. Collaboratively develop risk mitigation and contingency plans to address complex challenges.

4. Foster collaboration and knowledge sharing:

    - Encourage collaboration and knowledge sharing among project team members and stakeholders. Leverage their diverse expertise and perspectives to tackle complex problems collectively.

    - Establish mechanisms for cross-functional collaboration, such as workshops, brainstorming sessions, and communities of practice. Create opportunities for team members to learn from each other and leverage their collective intelligence.

5. Utilize adaptive project management approaches:

    - Embrace adaptive project management approaches, such as Agile or Lean, that are well-suited for complex and rapidly changing environments. These methodologies promote iterative development, flexibility, and continuous learning.

    - Break down the project into smaller, manageable components or iterations. Regularly review and adapt project plans and strategies based on emerging information, feedback, and evolving project dynamics.

6. Seek expert advice and guidance:

    - Recognize that navigating complexity may require specialized expertise or external insights. Seek advice and guidance from subject matter experts or consultants who have experience in managing complex projects.

    - Collaborate with professionals who can provide insights into specific domains, emerging technologies, or regulatory requirements. Leverage their expertise to make informed decisions and navigate complex challenges.

7. Foster adaptability and resilience:

- Cultivate a mindset of adaptability and resilience within the project team. Encourage team members to embrace change, learn from setbacks, and find innovative solutions to complex problems.

- Develop contingency plans and alternative strategies to respond to unexpected events or shifts in the project environment. Continuously monitor the project's progress and adjust plans as needed to navigate complexity effectively.

8. Communicate effectively:

- Establish clear and transparent communication channels to facilitate the flow of information and insights among stakeholders. Ensure that project progress, challenges, and complexities are effectively communicated.

- Adapt your communication style and methods to suit the diverse needs and preferences of different stakeholders. Provide regular updates, actively listen to concerns, and address questions related to project complexity.

9. Leverage technology and data:

    - Leverage technology tools and data analytics to gather insights, identify patterns, and make informed decisions in complex environments. Utilize project management software, data visualization tools, and analytics platforms to support decision-making.

    - Collect and analyze relevant data to gain a deeper understanding of project complexity and inform strategic decisions. Use data-driven insights to identify areas of improvement and optimize project performance.

10. Foster a learning culture:

    - Encourage a learning culture within the project team and organization. Emphasize the importance of continuous learning and improvement in navigating complexity. Here are some coaching tips to foster a learning culture:

        i. Promote knowledge sharing:

            a. Create platforms and opportunities for team members to share their knowledge, experiences, and lessons learned. Encourage the exchange of ideas, best practices, and insights related to navigating complexity.

b. Establish communities of practice or knowledge-sharing sessions where team members can discuss challenges, solutions, and innovative approaches to complex problems.

ii. Encourage experimentation and innovation:

a. Foster an environment where team members feel empowered to experiment with new ideas and approaches. Encourage them to explore innovative solutions to complex problems.

b. Celebrate and recognize team members who take calculated risks and generate valuable insights through experimentation. Encourage a mindset of continuous improvement and learning from both successes and failures.

iii. Provide learning resources and training:

a. Offer learning resources, training programs, and workshops that specifically address navigating complexity. Provide team members with access to relevant articles, books, online courses, and webinars.

b. Support team members in acquiring specialized skills and knowledge related to managing complexity. Consider sponsoring certifications or professional development opportunities to enhance their capabilities.

iv. Foster cross-functional collaboration:

a. Encourage collaboration across different functions and disciplines within the organization. Facilitate opportunities for team members to work on cross-functional projects or assignments that expose them to diverse perspectives and approaches.

b. Create a supportive environment where team members can learn from each other's experiences and leverage their collective expertise in navigating complexity.

v. Encourage reflection and debriefing:

   a. Promote regular reflection and debriefing sessions after completing complex project milestones or phases. Encourage team members to reflect on the challenges faced, lessons learned, and strategies employed.

   b. Facilitate discussions to identify areas of improvement, best practices, and opportunities for enhancing future project performance. Encourage open and honest conversations to foster a culture of learning and continuous improvement.

vi. Support mentorship and coaching:

   a. Establish mentorship and coaching programs within the organization. Pair experienced project managers with less experienced ones to provide guidance and support in navigating complexity.

   b. Encourage mentors and coaches to share their knowledge, insights, and strategies for managing complexity. Provide opportunities for mentees to seek advice, discuss challenges, and learn from their mentors' experiences.

vii. Recognize and celebrate learning achievements:

a. Celebrate individual and team achievements in navigating complexity and applying new learning. Recognize and reward team members who demonstrate a commitment to continuous learning, innovation, and effective management of complex projects.

b. Highlight success stories and lessons learned in project reviews, team meetings, or organizational newsletters. This promotes a culture where learning from complexity becomes an integral part of project management practices.

Remember, navigating complexity requires a mindset of continuous learning and adaptation. By fostering a learning culture, you enable your team members to develop the skills, knowledge, and resilience needed to navigate complex project environments successfully.

CHAPTER 10: COMPLEXITY

PRINCIPLE 10: OPTIMIZE RISK RESPONSES

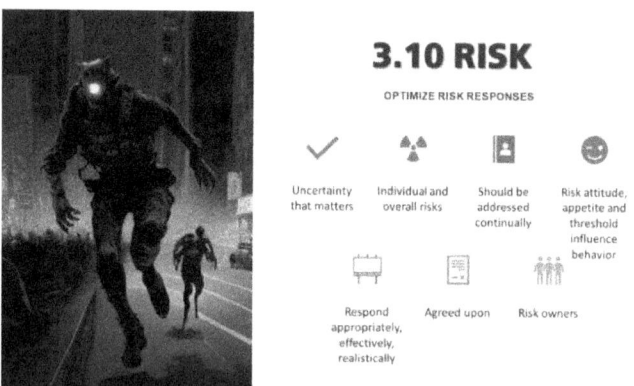

3.10 Optimize Risk Responses: This principle emphasizes the importance of optimizing risk responses to ensure that the project's objectives are achieved while minimizing negative impact.

Key Concepts:
- Continue to evaluate exposure to risk (positive and negative) both opportunities and threats to maximize positive impacts and minimize negative impacts to the project and its outcomes.
- Individual and overall risks can impact projects. Risk can be positive or negative. Risks are addressed continually throughout the project.

- An organization's risk attitude appetite and threshold influence how risk is addressed.

- What do we mean by appetite? Well how much food are you willing to eat?

- The question "How much risk are you willing to take on to pursue an opportunity?" describes appetite.

- Risk responses for both risks and opportunities, positive risk and negative risks should be appropriate for the significance of the risk, cost-effective realistic, and agreed to by relevant stakeholders. They should be owned by a responsible person usually known as the risk owner.

The Time Machine Project (Risk)

Mary understood that risks were inevitable in such a complex project. She proactively identified and assessed risks, considering their potential impacts on cost, schedule, and the successful completion of the time machine.

Through careful analysis, Mary and her team developed robust risk response plans. They implemented mitigation strategies to minimize the likelihood and impact of identified risks. They also prepared contingency plans, ensuring they were well-prepared to respond to any unforeseen events.

Regular risk reviews and monitoring were conducted to ensure that the risk response plans remained effective and aligned with the project's evolving dynamics. Mary engaged stakeholders in risk discussions, garnering their insights and support in mitigating risks effectively.

As the project advanced, unforeseen complexities and risks surfaced. Mary and her team remained agile and adaptable in their response. They drew upon their collective expertise and experience to adjust their risk response strategies as needed, addressing emerging risks and seizing opportunities.

Mary also understood that risk management was not solely about mitigating negative outcomes but also about capitalizing on positive possibilities. She encouraged the team to identify and exploit opportunities that arose from the project's complexities. By taking calculated risks, they were able to push the boundaries of what was thought possible, leading to breakthroughs and advancements.

Through their diligent navigation of complexity and optimization of risk responses, Mary and her team overcame significant challenges. Their ability to embrace complexity, collaborate effectively, and manage risks propelled the time machine project forward, inching closer to its ultimate realization.

Self-Retrospective

Effective risk management is crucial for project success, particularly in complex and uncertain environments. The principle of optimizing risk responses emphasizes the need to proactively identify, assess, and respond to risks in a way that maximizes opportunities and minimizes threats. Here are advanced coaching tips to optimize risk responses in your projects:

1. Develop a comprehensive risk management strategy:

    - Create a robust risk management strategy that outlines the processes, roles, and responsibilities for managing risks throughout the project lifecycle. Define clear objectives and criteria for risk assessment, prioritization, and response planning.

    - Establish a risk management framework that integrates seamlessly with project planning, execution, and control processes. Ensure that risk management activities are aligned with project objectives and overall organizational goals.

"and overall organizational goals." continue

ChatGPT

2. Foster a risk-aware culture:

    - Cultivate a risk-aware culture within the project team and organization. Encourage open and transparent communication about risks and their potential impact on project objectives.

- Promote proactive risk identification and reporting at all levels. Encourage team members to speak up about potential risks and encourage them to share their insights and expertise in managing risks.

3. Involve stakeholders in risk management:

    - Engage relevant stakeholders in the risk management process. Seek their input and perspectives during risk identification, analysis, and response planning.

    - Regularly communicate risk status and updates to stakeholders, ensuring that they are aware of the potential impact of risks on the project. Collaborate with stakeholders to develop effective risk response strategies and ensure their buy-in and support.

4. Apply a proactive approach to risk identification:

    - Adopt a proactive approach to risk identification by considering a wide range of potential risks. Encourage team members to think critically and creatively about risks that may arise during the project lifecycle.

- Utilize various techniques such as brainstorming, risk checklists, scenario analysis, and lessons learned from previous projects to identify risks. Encourage team members to share their diverse perspectives and experiences to uncover potential risks.

5. Conduct thorough risk analysis:

    - Perform comprehensive risk analysis to assess the potential impact and likelihood of identified risks. Utilize qualitative and quantitative risk analysis techniques to prioritize risks based on their significance.

    - Consider the interdependencies between risks and the potential cascading effects they may have on the project. Analyze risks from multiple dimensions, including technical, organizational, financial, and operational aspects.

6. Develop effective risk response strategies:

    - Develop risk response strategies that are aligned with project objectives and the identified risks. Consider a range of response options, including risk avoidance, mitigation, transfer, or acceptance.

- Prioritize response strategies based on their effectiveness, feasibility, and potential impact on project outcomes. Develop contingency plans for high-impact risks to minimize their consequences and ensure project continuity.

7. Implement proactive risk mitigation measures:

    - Implement proactive risk mitigation measures to reduce the likelihood or impact of identified risks. Assign responsibilities for executing risk mitigation actions and monitor their progress.

    - Implement controls and safeguards to mitigate risks effectively. Develop risk mitigation plans that are practical, realistic, and within the project's constraints.

8. Leverage opportunities within risks:

    - Adopt a positive mindset towards risks and identify potential opportunities within them. Analyze risks to uncover any positive outcomes or benefits that may arise if they are managed effectively.

    - Develop strategies to exploit these opportunities, such as leveraging new technologies, entering new markets, or improving project efficiency. Balance risk responses to maximize opportunities while mitigating threats.

9. Monitor and control risks:

- Establish a robust risk monitoring and control system to track the status of identified risks throughout the project. Regularly review and update risk registers and risk management plans.

- Implement mechanisms to monitor early warning signs and trigger appropriate risk responses. Develop risk response triggers and thresholds to guide timely and effective actions.

10. Learn from risk management experiences:

- Foster a culture of learning from risk management experiences. Encourage project team members to document lessons learned from managing risks and share them with the wider organization.

- Conduct post-project reviews to evaluate the effectiveness of risk responses and identify areas for improvement in future projects. Continuously refine risk management processes based on lessons learned and emerging best practices.

By optimizing risk responses, you proactively address potential threats and capitalize on opportunities, ultimately improving project outcomes. Effective risk management instills confidence in stakeholders, enhances project performance, and contributes to the achievement of organizational goals.

CHAPTER 11: COMPLEXITY

PRINCIPLE 11: EMBRACE ADAPTABILITY AND RESILIENCY

3.11 ADAPTABILITY AND RESILIENCY

EMBRACE ADAPTABILITY AND RESILIENCY

Adaptability: ability to respond to change

Resiliency: Ability to absorb impacts/recover

Focus on outcomes facilitates adaptability

3.11 Embrace Adaptability and Resiliency: This principle emphasizes the importance of embracing adaptability and resiliency in the face of change. This includes being flexible and adaptable to change while still maintaining project goals.

Key Concepts:
- Adaptability is the ability to respond to changing conditions.
- Resiliency is the ability to absorb impacts and to recover quickly from a setback or failure

- A focus on outcomes rather than outputs facilitates adaptability, so build adaptability and resiliency into the organizations and the project team's approaches to help the project accommodate change recover from setbacks and advance the work of the project.

- One of the ways to do this is to have your eyes and ears open to those internal and external environmental factors to be able to bounce back accordingly

The Time Machine Project (Adaptability and Resiliency)

The time machine project faced numerous unexpected challenges and uncertainties. Mary understood that adaptability and resiliency were crucial for overcoming these obstacles.

She fostered a mindset of adaptability within the team, encouraging them to be open to change and to embrace new ideas and approaches. When unforeseen circumstances arose, Mary led the team in assessing the situation, identifying alternative solutions, and adjusting plans accordingly.

Throughout the project, Mary remained resilient in the face of adversity. She provided unwavering support to her team, helping them navigate difficulties and maintain their motivation. She celebrated small victories along the way, fostering a positive and resilient team spirit.

As the project encountered unexpected setbacks, Mary exemplified adaptability by encouraging the team to think creatively and explore alternative paths. They re-evaluated their strategies, leveraged their expertise, and pivoted when necessary. By embracing adaptability, they turned challenges into opportunities for growth and innovation.

Mary also understood the importance of resilience. She acknowledged that setbacks were a natural part of any complex project and that maintaining a resilient mindset was crucial for persevering. She encouraged the team to learn from setbacks, adapt quickly, and keep their focus on the ultimate goal.

In the face of unexpected delays or technical hurdles, Mary remained calm and composed, providing the team with the confidence and support they needed to stay resilient. She fostered a culture where setbacks were seen as learning experiences, enabling the team to bounce back stronger and more determined than before.

Self-Retrospective

"In today's" continue ever-changing and uncertain business landscape, the ability to embrace adaptability and resiliency is critical for project success. The principle of embracing adaptability and resiliency emphasizes the need for project managers to be flexible, agile, and responsive to change. Here are advanced coaching tips to embrace adaptability and resiliency in your projects:

1. Foster a culture of adaptability:

    - Cultivate a culture that embraces change and encourages adaptability within the project team and organization. Help team members understand the importance of being open to new ideas, approaches, and perspectives.

    - Encourage a growth mindset where team members view challenges as opportunities for learning and growth. Foster an environment that rewards creativity, innovation, and the willingness to explore new possibilities.

2. Embrace iterative and incremental approaches:

   - Adopt iterative and incremental approaches, such as Agile or Lean methodologies, to enhance adaptability and responsiveness. Break down the project into smaller, manageable iterations or phases.

   - Regularly review and adjust project plans, priorities, and strategies based on feedback, emerging information, and changing stakeholder needs. Emphasize continuous improvement and learning throughout the project lifecycle.

3. Develop a flexible project management framework:

   - Establish a flexible project management framework that allows for adjustments and course corrections as the project progresses. Define clear change management processes and procedures to manage changes effectively.

   - Encourage the use of change control boards or similar mechanisms to evaluate and prioritize requested changes. Ensure that changes are assessed for their impact on project objectives, timelines, costs, and risks before implementation.

4. Proactively anticipate and manage change:

   - Develop a proactive change management strategy that includes tools and techniques for identifying, analyzing, and responding to potential changes. Encourage team members to be vigilant and proactive in identifying emerging trends, market shifts, and technological advancements that may impact the project.

   - Anticipate potential risks and opportunities associated with change and develop contingency plans or alternative strategies to address them. Engage stakeholders in change management activities and communicate the rationale behind changes effectively.

5. Build a resilient project team:

   - Invest in developing a resilient project team that can adapt to unforeseen circumstances and overcome challenges. Foster an environment of trust, collaboration, and psychological safety where team members feel supported in taking calculated risks and learning from failures.

- Provide training and development opportunities to enhance team members' skills and competencies related to adaptability, resilience, and change management. Encourage cross-training and skill diversification to ensure flexibility within the team.

6. Encourage effective communication and stakeholder engagement:

    - Establish robust communication channels to keep stakeholders informed about project changes, progress, and potential impacts. Proactively engage stakeholders in discussions and decision-making processes related to changes.

    - Tailor communication approaches to suit the needs and preferences of different stakeholders. Use clear and concise language, visual aids, and storytelling techniques to effectively convey the rationale behind changes and manage stakeholder expectations.

7. Develop contingency and fallback plans:

    - Create contingency and fallback plans to mitigate the impact of potential disruptions or setbacks. Identify alternative approaches, resources, or suppliers that can be leveraged in case of unexpected events.

- Continuously monitor the project's external environment for potential threats or opportunities. Develop early warning systems or triggers to prompt proactive responses and ensure project resiliency.

8. Encourage innovation and experimentation:

    - Foster a culture of innovation and experimentation within the project team. Encourage team members to explore new ideas, technologies, and approaches that can enhance project outcomes and adaptability.

    - Provide resources and support for piloting and testing innovative solutions. Encourage the documentation and sharing of lessons learned from successful experiments and failures to promote continuous learning and improvement.

9. Develop personal adaptability skills:

    - As a project manager, continuously develop your personal adaptability skills to serve as a role model for your team. Here are some ways to enhance your personal adaptability:

- Embrace a growth mindset: Adopt a mindset that views challenges as opportunities for growth and learning. Be open to new ideas, feedback, and perspectives, and seek continuous self-improvement.

- Cultivate self-awareness: Reflect on your own strengths, weaknesses, and areas for growth. Understand how your behavior and reactions impact the project team and stakeholders. Continuously seek feedback to gain insights into areas where you can enhance your adaptability.

- Enhance your problem-solving skills: Develop strong problem-solving and critical-thinking abilities. Practice analyzing complex situations, identifying potential solutions, and making informed decisions in dynamic and uncertain environments.

- Develop emotional intelligence: Improve your ability to understand and manage your emotions and those of others. Enhance your empathy, active listening, and conflict resolution skills to build positive relationships and navigate challenging situations effectively.

- Expand your knowledge and skills: Stay up to date with the latest industry trends, best practices, and emerging technologies. Continuously seek opportunities to expand your knowledge base and acquire new skills that are relevant to the changing project landscape.

- Be flexible and adaptable in your approach: Embrace flexibility in your project management approach. Be willing to adjust plans, timelines, and strategies as needed. Anticipate and plan for potential changes and have alternative solutions in place.

- Foster a learning mindset: Continuously seek opportunities for learning and development. Engage in professional networks, attend conferences, participate in workshops, and leverage online resources to enhance your knowledge and skills.

- Seek diverse perspectives: Encourage diversity of thought and seek input from team members and stakeholders with different backgrounds and experiences. Embrace different viewpoints to foster creativity, innovation, and adaptability.

- Stay resilient in the face of challenges: Build your resilience to effectively navigate setbacks, unexpected events, and ambiguity. Develop coping mechanisms, practice self-care, and maintain a positive mindset to bounce back from challenges and inspire your team to do the same.

By continuously developing your personal adaptability skills, you will be better equipped to lead your team through change and uncertainty, demonstrating resilience and inspiring others to embrace adaptability as well.

Finally, let's explore the principle of enabling change to achieve the envisioned future state.

CHAPTER 12: CHANGE

PRINCIPLE 12: ENABLE CHANGE TO ACHIEVE THE ENVISIONED FUTURE STATE

3.12 Enable Change to Achieve the Envisioned Future State: This principle emphasizes the importance of enabling change to achieve the envisioned future state. This includes the ability to create a vision, develop a plan, and implement change to achieve project goals

Key Concepts:
- A structured approach to change helps individuals' groups and the organization transition from the current state to a future desired state, after all that's what projects are all about! Moving from a current state to a future state!

- Change can originate from internal influences or external sources.

- Enabling change can be challenging as not all stakeholders embrace change.

- Attempting too much change in a short time can lead to change fatigue and resistance.

- Stakeholder engagement and motivational approaches assist in change adoption.

- Prepare those impacted for the adoption and sustainment of new and different behaviors and processes required for the transition from the current state to the intended future state created by the project outcomes.

- Have empathy for people

The Time Machine Project (Stewardship)

As the time machine project neared its completion, Mary focused on enabling change to achieve the envisioned future state. She communicated the project's progress and milestones to stakeholders, ensuring their understanding and support for the final stages.

Mary understood that successful implementation of the time machine required a comprehensive change management approach. She developed a detailed plan that addressed the technical, organizational, and human aspects of change. This included stakeholder engagement, communication strategies, and training programs.

She engaged stakeholders early on, ensuring their involvement and buy-in throughout the change process. Mary communicated the benefits of the time machine, highlighting how it would revolutionize the way we understand and explore time. She addressed any concerns or resistance, fostering a sense of excitement and anticipation for the future state.

Mary and her team developed comprehensive training programs to enable stakeholders to effectively utilize the time machine. They provided user documentation, conducted workshops, and offered support to ensure a smooth transition from project completion to operational readiness. By empowering stakeholders with the knowledge and skills to embrace the time machine, Mary ensured its successful implementation and adoption.

To facilitate change and streamline processes, Mary leveraged cutting-edge technology. She collaborated with an AI tool named Charlamagne, which helped coordinate activities, manage data, and optimize the overall project outcome. The AI tool served as a valuable resource, enhancing efficiency and enabling smooth change implementation.

Finally, the time machine project was successfully completed. The team had overcome challenges, built strong relationships, and navigated complexities. With Mary's leadership, adaptability, and resilience, they had created a groundbreaking invention that would redefine our understanding of time.

The envisioned future state had been achieved, and the time machine was poised to open new doors of discovery and exploration. The project stood as a testament to Mary's exemplary leadership, her ability to embrace change, and her unwavering commitment to realizing a visionary goal.

Self-Retrospective

In today's dynamic business environment, change is inevitable. The principle of enabling change emphasizes the importance of effectively managing and leading change initiatives to achieve the envisioned future state. Here are advanced coaching tips to enable change in your projects:

1. Develop a compelling vision:

    - Clearly articulate the vision of the future state that the project aims to achieve. Ensure that the vision is inspiring, realistic, and aligned with the strategic objectives of the organization.

    - Communicate the vision to stakeholders, emphasizing the benefits and opportunities that the change will bring. Create a shared understanding and commitment to the vision across the project team and stakeholders.

2. Establish a change management framework:

    - Develop a change management framework that outlines the processes, tools, and responsibilities for managing change throughout the project. Define clear roles and responsibilities for change management activities.

    - Integrate change management activities with project planning and execution processes. Ensure that change management plans are aligned with the project's objectives and overall organizational goals.

3. Engage and communicate with stakeholders:

    - Identify and engage key stakeholders early in the change process. Understand their needs, concerns, and expectations regarding the change. Develop tailored communication plans to address their specific needs.

    - Communicate the rationale for change, the benefits it brings, and how it aligns with the organization's goals. Provide regular updates on the progress of the change initiative and address any resistance or concerns proactively.

4. Build a change-ready culture within the project team and organization:

    - Foster a culture that values and embraces change. Communicate the importance of adaptability, innovation, and continuous improvement to all team members.

    - Encourage a growth mindset where individuals are open to new ideas, willing to take calculated risks, and see change as an opportunity for growth and development.

    - Promote a safe and supportive environment where team members feel comfortable expressing their opinions, providing feedback, and sharing their concerns related to the change.

    - Recognize and reward behaviors that demonstrate agility, resilience, and a positive attitude towards change. Celebrate successes and milestones achieved through the change process.

    - Provide training and development opportunities to enhance change management skills and competencies within the team. Equip team members with the necessary tools and techniques to navigate and lead change effectively.

- Encourage collaboration and cross-functional teamwork to break down silos and facilitate the exchange of ideas and knowledge. Foster a sense of collective ownership and responsibility for driving and implementing change.

- Lead by example as a change agent. Demonstrate a proactive and positive attitude towards change, embracing new approaches and encouraging others to do the same. Be visible, accessible, and supportive throughout the change process.

- Continuously communicate the purpose and benefits of the change initiative, keeping the team and stakeholders informed and engaged. Provide regular updates on progress, milestones achieved, and lessons learned.

- Create opportunities for team members to participate in the change process. Empower them to contribute their insights, ideas, and suggestions for improvement. Involve them in decision-making processes that directly impact the change initiative.

- Monitor and measure the effectiveness of change management efforts. Establish key performance indicators (KPIs) to track progress, evaluate the impact of the change, and identify areas for improvement. Use data and feedback to inform decision-making and course corrections as needed.

- Encourage a continuous learning and improvement mindset throughout the change journey. Reflect on lessons learned, document best practices, and incorporate feedback into future change initiatives.

By building a change-ready culture, you create an environment where the project team and organization are more adaptable, responsive, and resilient in the face of change. This enables successful implementation of the envisioned future state and sets the stage for continued growth and success.

In conclusion, the twelve principles of the Project Management Body of Knowledge (PMBOK) provide a comprehensive framework for project managers to excel in their roles and drive successful projects. By embracing these principles and applying advanced coaching techniques, project managers with 20 years of experience can elevate their leadership, vision, and impact across industries. From being diligent, respectful, and caring stewards to enabling change to achieve the envisioned future state, project managers can inspire their teams, engage stakeholders, and deliver exceptional results. Remember, the key lies in continuous learning, adaptation, and the application of these principles to your specific project context.

Epilogue: The Legacy of the Time Machine

The completion of the time machine marked a significant milestone in human history. Dr. Zakari's insatiable desire to explore the mysteries of time, combined with Mary's exceptional project management skills, had brought forth a scientific marvel.

The time machine's unveiling captivated the world, garnering widespread attention and fascination.

People from all corners of the globe marveled at the possibility of traveling through time, envisioning the endless opportunities it could unlock. News outlets, scientists, and enthusiasts all clamored to witness the inaugural journey of the time machine.

The event was carefully orchestrated to ensure maximum impact. World leaders, renowned scientists, and influential figures were invited to witness the historic moment. Mary and her team took pride in showcasing their accomplishment, knowing that their hard work and dedication had resulted in a groundbreaking achievement.

As the time machine whirred to life, anticipation filled the air. The world held its breath as the first travelers stepped into the machine, ready to embark on a journey through time. Cameras flashed, capturing the moment for eternity.

The inaugural trip was a resounding success. The time machine transported its passengers to significant moments in history, allowing them to witness events that had shaped civilizations. From the pyramids of ancient Egypt to the signing of pivotal treaties, the time machine brought history to life.

But it didn't stop there. The time machine also offered glimpses into the future, sparking imaginations and igniting discussions about what lay ahead for humanity. People were filled with wonder and excitement as they contemplated the possibilities and contemplated the impact the time machine could have on the course of history.

In the wake of the time machine's success, the company behind the project flourished. Time travel experiences became a sought-after commodity, with individuals eager to explore the past and catch a glimpse of what the future held. The company's profits soared, allowing for further research and development of groundbreaking technologies.

The impact of the time machine extended beyond entertainment and tourism. Historians gained invaluable insights into the past, enhancing their understanding of key events and eras. Scientists utilized the time machine's capabilities to conduct groundbreaking experiments and study phenomena that were previously inaccessible.

As the world adapted to the new era ushered in by the time machine, Mary and her team remained at the forefront of innovation. Their expertise and experience became highly sought after, and they were often invited to speak at conferences and share their insights with the next generation of project managers.

The legacy of the time machine project endured, inspiring countless individuals to push the boundaries of what was deemed possible. The principles of project management that Mary and her team had embraced became guiding beacons for project managers worldwide, fostering a culture of diligence, collaboration, and innovation.

With each passing year, the time machine's impact continued to reverberate. Its influence extended beyond the realms of science and technology, shaping the way humanity perceived time and the possibilities it held. It became a symbol of human ingenuity, reminding people that with vision, dedication, and effective project management, extraordinary achievements could be realized.

And so, as the world embarked on a new era of discovery and exploration, the completion of the time machine stood as a testament to the power of human potential. The story of Mary, Dr. Zakari, and their remarkable team would be forever etched in the annals of history, inspiring generations to come to dream big, embrace challenges, and reach for the stars. The completion of the time machine was not just the end of a project; it was the beginning of a new chapter in the ongoing quest for knowledge and progress.

PHILL AKINWALE, PMP, CSM, PSM, ACP, PAL

CHAPTER SEVEN: QUIZ TIME

1. Project examples could include which of the following?
   A. Publication of a children's book
   B. Covid-19 vaccine
   C. Human beings landing on the moon
   D. All of the above

2. The *PMBOK® Guide* and the Standard for Project Management are both in one book.

12 PROJECT MANAGEMENT PRINCIPLES

   A. True

   B. False

3. A _____ is a temporary endeavor undertaken to create a unique product, service, or result.

   A. Project

   B. Operation

   C. Program

   D. Portfolio

4. Fulfillment of project objectives may produce which of the following?

   A. A product that is not unique and can be either a component of another item

   B. A non-unique service or a capability to perform a service

   C. A unique result, such as an outcome or document

   D. A repetitive task to add value to produce a repeat product or service

5. Examples of projects include which of the following?

   A. Expanding a tour guide service and merging two organizations

B. Improving a business process within an organization

C. Acquiring a hardware system and exploring for oil in a region

D. All of the options

6. Projects, programs, subsidiary portfolios, and operations managed as a group to achieve strategic objectives. What does this describe?

A. Project
B. Operation
C. Program
D. Portfolio

7. _____ is concerned with the ongoing production of goods and/or services. It ensures that business operations continue efficiently by using the optimal resources needed to meet customer demands.

A. Project management
B. Operations management
C. Program management
D. Portfolio management

8. What is a document established by an authority, custom, or general consent as a model or example known as?

A. Standard

B. Regulation

C. Legal Restriction

D. Governmental agency rule

9. Which of the following moves an organization from one state to another?

A. Project

B. Process

C. Procedure

D. Benefit

10. The benefit that the results of a specific project provide to its stakeholders is known as _____

A. Business value

B. Benefits management

C. Stockholder equity

D. Strategic alignment

11. An agile approach to planning_____.

A. Results in plans that encourage change and that are easily changed
B. Focuses on the plan documents rather than the planning process
C. Results in a fully defined schedule and budget
D. Fully defines product features early in the project

12. Agile is best used when _____
A. There is low variability is needed on the project
B. Change is unlikely and static requirements are needed
C. Experimentation and discovery are needed for the solution
D. Little chance of change and high certainty

13. Which of the following is most important on all projects?
    - *Deliver on Time*
    - *Deliver on Budget*
    - *Deliver all Planned Scope*
    - *Meet Customer Needs*
    - *Meet Quality Requirements*
    - *Team Satisfaction*

A. Time

B. Budget

C. The 3 lower-level items on the list

D. The 3 higher level items on the list

14. Which of these is NOT a function associated with a project?

   A. Provide oversight and coordination

   B. Present objectives and feedback

   C. Control the company revenues

   D. Perform work and contribute insights

15. External environments include:

   A. Infrastructure

   B. Academic research

   C. Information technology software

   D. Resource availability and commercial databases

16. The PMI® Code of Ethics includes _____ (select all that apply)

   A. Responsibility and Respect

   B. Respect and Bureaucracy

   C. Resiliency and Responsibility

   D. Fairness and Respect

17. The first principle about stewardship includes:

A. Integrity and Rewards

B. Care and Remuneration

C. Trustworthiness and Compliance

D. All of the options

18. The second principle encourages a _____ team environment.

A. Communicative

B. Collaborative

C. Participative

D. Conniving

19. Stakeholder engagement is _____ for success

A. A bit important

B. Not important

C. Critical

D. Subjective

20. According to PMI, value is _____ and driver of projects.

A. The ultimate success indicator

B. The monetary indicator

C. Tangible

D. Quantifiable

21. According to PMI:

    A. A project is a system

    B. Systems occasionally change

    C. A project is not a system

    D. Systems thinking is a partial view

22. Which of these terms best describes leadership?

A. Authority

B. Position

C. Title

D. Influence

23. According to PMI, tailoring is _____

A. Iterative

B. Continuous

C. A constant process

D. All of the above

24. According to PMI, quality involves _____

A. Aggravating stakeholders

B. Meeting acceptance criteria

C. Ensuring project processes are inappropriate

D. All of the options

25. According to PMI, complexity is the result of _____

A. Human behavior

B. System interactions

C. Uncertainty and ambiguity

D. All of the options

26. Project risk management should be _____

A. Appropriate to the significance of the risk

B. Cost effective in meeting personal goals and targets

C. Realistic within the operations context

D. Disagreed upon by all parties

27. Resiliency is best described as the _____

A. Ability to respond to change

B. Ability to absorb impacts/recover

C. Ability to configure a project

D. Ability to focus on project outcomes

28. According to PMI, too much change _____

A. Could lead to over-energizing the team
B. Could lead to change fatigue and resistance
C. Could help enable stakeholder engagement
D. Is not possible because change always contributes

29. You are working on a project with low requirements uncertainty and a low technical uncertainty. Due to these low levels of uncertainty, which model should you select?

A. Hybrid
B. Agile
C. Iterative
D. Predictive

30. Which of the following factors typically does not influence the nature of project delivery method selected?

A. Deliverable
B. Organization
C. Project
D. Motivation and machines

PHILL AKINWALE, PMP, CSM, PSM, ACP, PAL

Final Project Management Quiz Answers

1. **Project examples could include which of the following?**
   A. Publication of a children's book
   B. Covid-19 vaccine
   C. Human beings landing on the moon
   D. All of the above
   Answer: D
   Rationale: all the options are correct. They are all examples of a project; temporary, unique, and they start and an end.

2. **The *PMBOK® Guide* and the Standard for Project Management are both in one book.**
   A. True
   B. False
   Answer: A
   Rationale: this is true. The *PMBOK® Guide* is made up of two parts.

3. **A _____ is a temporary endeavor undertaken to create a unique product, service, or result.**
   A. Project
   B. Operation
   C. Program

D. Portfolio

Answer: A

Rationale: This defines a project.

4. **Fulfillment of project objectives may produce which of the following?**
   A. A product that is not unique and can be either a component of another item
   B. A non-unique service or a capability to perform a service
   C. **A unique result, such as an outcome or document**
   D. A repetitive task to add value to produce a repeat product or service

Answer: C

Rationale: This describes what a project could produce.

5. **Examples of projects include which of the following?**
   A. Expanding a tour guide service and merging two organizations
   B. Improving a business process within an organization
   C. Acquiring a hardware system and exploring for oil in a region
   D. **All of the options**

Answer: D

Rationale: all the options are correct. They are all examples of a project; temporary, unique, and they start and an end.

6. Projects, programs, subsidiary portfolios, and operations managed as a group to achieve strategic objectives. What does this describe?
A. Project
B. Operation
C. Program
D. Portfolio

Answer: D

Rationale: this defines a portfolio.

7. _____ is concerned with the ongoing production of goods and/or services. It ensures that business operations continue efficiently by using the optimal resources needed to meet customer demands.
A. Project management
B. Operations management
C. Program management
D. Portfolio management

Answer: B

Rationale: this defines operations management.

8. What is a document established by an authority, custom, or general consent as a model or example known as?
A. Standard
B. Regulation
C. Legal Restriction
D. Governmental agency rule

Answer: A
Rationale: this defines a standard.

9. **Which of the following moves an organization from one state to another?**
A. **Project**
B. Process
C. Procedure
D. Benefit
Answer: A
Rationale: the best answer is project.

10. **The benefit that the results of a specific project provide to its stakeholders is known as** _____
A. **Business value**
B. Benefits management
C. Stockholder equity
D. Strategic alignment
Answer: A
Rationale: the best answer is business value.

11. **An agile approach to planning** _____.
A. **Results in plans that encourage change and that are easily changed**
B. Focuses on the plan documents rather than the planning process
C. Results in a fully defined schedule and budget
D. Fully defines product features early in the project
Answer: A

Rationale: Agile results in plans that encourage change and that are easily changed. Agile is a change-based approach – adaptive, not prescriptive

12. Agile is best used when _____
    A. There is low variability is needed on the project
    B. Change is unlikely and static requirements are needed
    C. Experimentation and discovery are needed for the solution
    D. Little chance of change and high certainty

Answer: C
Rationale: Agile is best used when experimentation and discovery are needed for the solution.

13. Which of the following is most important on all projects?
    - *Deliver on Time*
    - *Deliver on Budget*
    - *Deliver all Planned Scope*
    - *Meet Customer Needs*
    - *Meet Quality Requirements*
    - *Team Satisfaction*

    A. Time
    B. Budget
    C. The 3 lower-level items on the list
    D. The 3 higher level items on the list
    Answer: C

12 PROJECT MANAGEMENT PRINCIPLES

Rationale: the most important elements on all projects revolve around the team, customer and quality. The other elements are not unimportant, but people elements should come first. As the Agile Manifesto states: Individuals and interactions over processes and tools.

14. Which of these is NOT a function associated with
    a project?
    A. Provide oversight and coordination
    B. Present objectives and feedback
    C. Control the company revenues
    D. Perform work and contribute insights
    Answer: C
    Rationale: this is not one of the functions associated with a project.

15. External environments include:
    A. Infrastructure
    B. Academic research
    C. Information technology software
    D. Resource availability and commercial databases
    Answer: B
    Rationale: this is not one of the functions associated with a project.

16. The PMI® Code of Ethics includes _____ (select all that apply)
    A. Responsibility and Respect
    B. Respect and Bureaucracy

C. Resiliency and Responsibility
D. Fairness and Respect
Answer: A and D
Rationale: the PMI Code of Ethics includes Responsibility, Respect, Fairness and Honesty.

17. **The first principle about stewardship includes:**
    A. Integrity and Rewards
    B. Care and Remuneration
    C. Trustworthiness and Compliance
    D. All of the options
    Answer: C
    Rationale: the first principle about stewardship includes trustworthiness and compliance.

18. **The second principle encourages a _____ team environment.**
    A. Communicative
    B. Collaborative
    C. Participative
    D. Conniving
    Answer: B
    Rationale: the second principle encourages a collaborative team environment.

19. **Stakeholder engagement is _____ for success**
    A. A bit important
    B. Not important
    C. Critical

D. Subjective

Answer: C

Rationale: stakeholder engagement is critical for success.

20. According to PMI, value is _____ and driver of projects.
A. **The ultimate success indicator**
B. The monetary indicator
C. Tangible
D. Quantifiable

Answer: A

Rationale: value is the ultimate success indicator.

21. According to PMI:
A. **A project is a system**
B. Systems occasionally change
C. A project is not a system
D. Systems thinking is a partial view

Answer: A

Rationale: A project is a system.

22. Which of these terms best describes leadership?
A. Authority
B. Position
C. Title
D. **Influence**

Answer: D

Rationale: the true measure of leadership is influence (John C. Maxwell). Although one's position, title and authority are a starting point for any leader, the word the best sums it up is influence.

23. According to PMI, tailoring is _____
A. Iterative
B. Continuous
C. A constant process
D. All of the above
Answer: D
Rationale: all the options describe the nature of tailoring.

24. According to PMI, quality involves _____
A. Aggravating stakeholders
B. Meeting acceptance criteria
C. Ensuring project processes are inappropriate
D. All of the options
Answer: B
Rationale: the best option is meeting acceptance criteria.

25. According to PMI, complexity is the result of _____
A. Human behavior
B. System interactions
C. Uncertainty and ambiguity
D. All of the options
Answer: D
Rationale: all the options are correct. Complexity is the result of all 3 options.

12 PROJECT MANAGEMENT PRINCIPLES

26.   Project risk management should be _____

A. **Appropriate to the significance of the risk**
B. Cost effective in meeting personal goals and targets
C. Realistic within the operations context
D. Disagreed upon by all parties

Answer: A

Rationale: the best option is "appropriate to the significance of the risk". The question is about projects not operations or personal goals.

27. Resiliency is best described as the _____

A. Ability to respond to change
B. **Ability to absorb impacts/recover**
C. Ability to configure a project
D. Ability to focus on project outcomes

Answer: B

Rationale: this is the best description of resiliency. Ability to absorb impacts/recover.

28.   According to PMI, too much change _____

A. Could lead to over-energizing the team
B. **Could lead to change fatigue and resistance**
C. Could help enable stakeholder engagement
D. Is not possible because change always contributes

Answer: B

Rationale: the best option is "too much change could lead to change fatigue and resistance."

29. You are working on a project with low requirements uncertainty and a low technical uncertainty. Due to these low levels of uncertainty, which model should you select?
A. Hybrid
B. Agile
C. Iterative
D. Predictive
Answer: D
Rationale: based on the Stacey Complexity Model, the best option is Predictive.

30. Which of the following factors typically does not influence the nature of project delivery method selected?
A. Deliverable
B. Organization
C. Project
D. Motivation and machines
Answer: D
Rationale: motivation and machines does not influence of project delivery method selected.

About the Author

Phill C. Akinwale, PMP has managed operational endeavors, projects and project controls across government and private sectors in various companies, including Motorola, Honeywell, Emerson, Skillsoft, Citigroup, Iron Mountain, Brown and Caldwell, US Airways and CVS Caremark. With his extensive experience in various facets of Project Management and rigorous project controls, he has trained project management worldwide (NASA, FBI, USAF, USACE, US Army, Department of Transport) across five PMBOK® Guide editions over the last 15 years.

He holds twelve project management certifications with six in Agile Project Management (CSM, PMI-ACP, PSM, PSPO, PAL, SPS). As a John Maxwell Certified Coach and Speaker, Phill delivers workshops, seminars, keynote speaking, and coaching in leadership and soft skills. Working together with you and your team or organization, he will guide you in the desired direction and equip you to reach your goals. Books he has authored include: The No-Good Leader, Earned Value Basics and Project Management Mid-Level to C-Level.

www.ingramcontent.com/pod-product-compliance
Lightning Source LLC
Chambersburg PA
CBHW071850230426
43671CB00012B/2129